BEHIND CLOSED DOORS

BEHIND CLOSED DOORS

A Handbook On How To Pray

Joseph M. Champlin

Paulist Press
New York/Ramsey

Acknowledgments

The English translation of the General Instruction for the Liturgy of the Hours is taken from *Documents on the Liturgy, 1963–1979: Conciliar, Papal, and Curial Texts* © 1982, International Committee on English in the Liturgy, Inc. ICEL. All rights reserved. Excerpts from *Centering Prayer* by M. Basil Pennington, copyright © 1980 by Cistercian Abbey of Spencer, Inc., are reprinted by permission of Doubleday & Co. Inc.

NIHIL OBSTAT
Rev. David W. Barry

IMPRIMATUR
+ Francis J. Harrison
Bishop of Syracuse

June 15, 1984

The *Nihil Obstat* and *Imprimatur* are official declarations that a book or pamphlet is free of doctrinal or moral error. No implication is contained therein that those who have granted the *Nihil Obstat* and *Imprimatur* agree with the contents, opinions or statements expressed.

Library of Congress Catalog Card Number: 84-80356

ISBN: 0-8091-2637-0

Published by Paulist Press
545 Island Road, Ramsey, N.J. 07446

Printed and bound in the
United States of America

Contents

Introduction

I would like to begin with a short quiz.

Question: Why would a book on prayer carry the title *Behind Closed Doors?*

Response: Because Jesus said, "Whenever you pray, go to your room, close your door, and pray to your Father in private" (Matthew 6:6).

Comment: That would be a logical and good explanation, but it is not the reason for the title.

Response: Because of the resurrection evening event in which Jesus appeared to the disciples who "had locked the doors of the place where they were for fear of the Jews" (John 20:19–20).

Comment: That, too, would be a very suitable motive, but it is not the one either.

Response: Because Jesus "often retired to deserted places and prayed" and we, like the Master, sometimes seek similar secluded areas to step aside and rest awhile in quiet prayer.

Comment: That is nearest to the actual reason so far, but it still falls short.

Response: Because in prayer we bring out matters locked up inside us and take them to God.

Comment: That certainly is a definite part of proper prayer, but neither is it the accurate explanation.

Response: Because of a current song with the same title.

Comment: I haven't heard the tune, but better informed music people tell me that this definitely could not be the motivation for *Behind Closed Doors.*

Are you growing weary of the quiz?

Those suggested spiritual reasons for the title are excellent indeed, and I hope the phrase *Behind Closed Doors* will trigger in the minds and hearts of readers such images and thoughts as they move through the book. Nevertheless, *Behind Closed Doors* has a quite different and rather earthy origin. I now will explain how this handbook on prayer and its title came into being.

1

On eleven evenings during Lent of 1983, I loaded up my orange Fiesta with several cartons of books, pamphlets and fliers, drove to different locations throughout the diocese of Syracuse and conducted workshops simply called "How To Pray."

These evenings, substantially identical in content, but repeated at various cities or towns for the convenience of our people, drew an average of seventy persons, with the smallest crowd around fifty and the largest approximating one hundred and fifty. The participants were interested, serious and joyful individuals quite content to spend three hours hearing about and experiencing diverse kinds of prayer.

This book developed out of those sessions. Like the workshops, it begins with seven general principles about prayer, although explained here in more detail. The text, also like the evening conferences, then moves on to describe in a concise, practical manner seven ways of praying. It concludes with an appendix containing excerpts from the General Instruction for the Liturgy of the Hours which is an extremely rich treatise on prayer as well as a complete set of directions on how to use the Church's official prayer book.

At those night sessions we did not merely talk about prayer; we actually experienced several types of praying, in particular meditation and centering prayer. This book has been written with a similar purpose in mind. The chapters are for the most part of modest length and prefaced with biblical quotations. I hope readers will choose to take them in single, day by day bites, perhaps with Bibles by their sides. After finishing a chapter, they might then spend some moments pondering the content with the reflective prayer suggestions at the end as aids.

Behind Closed Doors thus, as the subtitle states, is more of a manual or handbook for continual and repetitious use than a "read it through at one sitting" publication.

The title, and here is the answer to my quiz, also grew out of those Lenten workshops. During one session early on in the series I inquired from the almost totally lay audience where they normally found a still spot for prayer or what they had discovered to be the best location for a few minutes alone with God. The answer, hesitatingly offered by one participant, but then laughingly reinforced by at least half of the others present, was the bathroom. At all the subsequent meetings, I heard a majority of the crowd confirm with their nodding and smiling heads this perhaps surprising truth.

Later, too, many lay persons have in personal conversations reinforced the point for me, describing specifically how within a crowded and busy household it is often only behind the closed door of the bathroom that they find moments of quiet space for prayer.

Did those workshops bear much spiritual fruit and produce any measurable results? Only God, of course, knows and evaluates the total inner prayer life of a person. We humans can only judge by externals. Nevertheless, when participation for a few hours at one session on a weekday night immediately led to substantial and observable behavioral changes in many people's way of praying, then something quite good obviously happened at the workshops.

Two letters among others, received shortly after these sessions concluded, testify to such very concrete developments resulting from the "How To Pray" programs.

From Bainbridge, a small southern tier village of New York State, one wife and mother wrote:

> Your presentation on the subject of prayer given last Wednesday at St. Bartholomew's has helped me in a variety of ways. Now when my five year old leaves for school, I place the sign of the cross on her forehead and she does likewise to me! It puts us in a better frame of mind.
>
> When I take my walk at night I now say the Rosary by remembering someone for each bead. I use the Franciscan Crown and yet I still run out of beads before I can mention everyone.
>
> Meditating has become a more meaningful part of each day and is easier to do when I call to mind a Bible story.

From Camillus, a typical suburban section of Syracuse, one husband and father commented:

> My main difficulty is arranging for a quiet time and space. I have taken advantage of those few times when no one was home for Scripture meditation and spontaneous prayer.

I was interested in your comments on the Psalms, and how we can come to appreciate them and how they can grow on us. So, I have been trying to read one Psalm a day, slowly and reflectively. But I need more practice reflecting, since I either tend to become distracted, lack imagination, or fail to put forth the necessary effort. (Now I know what priests during all those years were reading, as they walked and read outdoors, wearing their birettas.)

I have tried centering prayer, but the places and times weren't the best. I think the major problem is to get myself to sit still and quietly in a place with no distractions. Occasionally when running, I've prayed this way, but after a while I realize I've been daydreaming or I get tired.

St. John Vianney, the Curé of Ars, prayed constantly and taught others how to pray. In a catechetical instruction found in the Liturgy of the Hours for his feast on August 4, he made these comments:

My little children, your hearts are small, but prayer stretches them and makes them capable of loving God. Through prayer we receive a foretaste of heaven and something of paradise comes down upon us. Prayer never leaves us without sweetness. It is honey that flows into the soul and makes all things sweet. When we pray properly, sorrows disappear like snow before the sun.

My own prayer is that readers will derive as much profit from these printed pages as the listeners, typified by the woman from Bainbridge and the man from Camillus, gained from those spoken words at the Lenten workshops. I hope *Behind Closed Doors* will become a frequently used manual on prayer which points out a path for beginners, opens up new horizons for those already a good distance along the way, and reinforces the efforts of people who have been praying for years. I would be delighted to learn in the months ahead that it has become very much like an old friend with whom we visit from time to time. I likewise will indeed be grateful to God if it develops into a helpful guide which enables users to pray better and leads to the kind of prayer that gives its practitioners a foretaste of heaven, a touch of paradise and a power capable of making sorrows disappear like snow before the sun.

I wish here to thank: Mr. Frank Cunningham for his initial encouragement and Mr. Ken Peters for his valuable recommendation about reflective prayer suggestions after each section; Monsignor A. Robert Casey, Rev. Robert Chryst, Mrs. Mary Ann Church, Mr. Walter Gilroy, and Sister Barbara Smith, D.C. for their careful reading and constructive criticisms of the text; Mrs. Patricia Gale, my efficient typist for the past five years, for remarkable deciphering of sometimes illegible handwriting; Mr. Don Brophy, my editor at Paulist Press, who at a crucial moment provided needed support and guidance; and, finally, the nearly eight hundred participants at those workshops who provided most of the inspiration, some of the content and the precise title for this book.

Part I:

Seven General Principles of Prayer

There is no one model or perfect way of praying. Just as we are each unique creations of God, so every individual will have her or his personal manner of best speaking and listening to the Lord. These general principles, however, apply to all types of prayer, including the very diverse methods described in Part II.

◊ *Principle # 1:*

We should pray constantly, but without some set aside solitude and silence each day, it will be impossible to achieve that goal.

The apostles returned to Jesus and reported to him all that they had done and what they had taught. He said to them, "Come by yourselves to an out-of-the-way place and rest a little." People were coming and going in great numbers, making it impossible for them to so much as eat. So Jesus and the apostles went off in the boat by themselves to a deserted place (Mark 6:30–32).

Father Henri Nouwen is one of America's more popular Catholic speakers and writers on the topic of prayer and spirituality. Very much in demand as a lecturer around this country and a prolific author, the European-born priest also in recent years has taught at Yale and Harvard, carried on extensive correspondence and counseled countless persons. In the midst of that busy life, however, he has at least twice temporarily dropped out of circulation, withdrawn from the mainstream of these activities and retired to a Trappist monastery for about six months of silence, prayer and reflection.

During those and other moments of solitude, Nouwen often pondered what St. Paul meant when he either urged Christians to pray constantly, always and without ceasing, or described how he did so for them.

For example, the apostle urges:

Rejoice always, never cease praying, render constant thanks; such is God's will for you in Christ Jesus (1 Thessalonians 5:16–18).

9

Rejoice in the Lord always! I say it again. Rejoice (Philippians 4:4).

At every opportunity pray in the Spirit, using prayers and petitions of every sort. Pray constantly and attentively for all in the holy company (Ephesians 6:18).

Paul also practiced what he preached:

I continually thank my God for you . . . (1 Corinthians 1:4).

It is no more than right that we thank God unceasingly for you . . . (2 Thessalonians 1:3).

We pray for you always . . . (2 Thessalonians 1:11).

Father Nouwen notes that two Greek words appear repeatedly in these types of Pauline exhortations or descriptions and they mean "always" or "without interruption."

According to Nouwen's analysis of those terms, St. Paul "does not exhort his readers to pray once in a while, regularly, or often, but without hesitation admonishes them to pray constantly, unceasingly, without interruption. Paul does not ask us to spend some of every day in prayer. No, Paul is more radical. He asks us to pray day and night, in joy and in sorrow, at work and at play, without intermission or breaks."[1]

What does that mean? How is it possible?

Struggling with those questions, Nouwen goes on at length to explain the difference between unceasing thought and unceasing prayer. He also suggests ways to achieve the goal or ideal of constant prayer. But Nouwen's practical conclusion simply reiterates and reinforces our first principle of prayer: "Those who do not set aside a certain place and time each day to do nothing else but pray can never expect their unceasing thought to become unceasing prayer."[2]

The always busy person who asserts "My work is my prayer" and who never withdraws from daily tasks for periods of explicit prayer walks a dangerous path. Such an individual should not seek support from the teaching or lives of well-known, active, zealous, hard laboring Christians from earliest days until the present. Neither St. Paul nor Archbishop Fulton J. Sheen would agree with that approach, nor would Mother Teresa ministering to the poorest of the poor in the slums of Calcutta or Reverend David Wilkerson reaching out to the teenagers in the asphalt jungle of New York City. Nor would our Master, Teacher and Model, the Lord Jesus. All of them made and make explicit time just for prayer each day.

The New Testament clearly portrays Jesus as a busy person and a ceaselessly working individual, a preacher and a doer. "He went about doing good works and healing all who were in the grip of the devil . . . " (Acts 10:38). "His reputation spread more and more, and great crowds gathered to hear him and to be cured of their maladies" (Luke 5:15). Moreover, Christ had much to accomplish and little time in which to complete his tasks.

Yet despite those various pressures, the Lord regularly and frequently found time and space for prayer.

It is interesting and inspiring to page through the Gospel according to Luke and note the many explicit references about Jesus and prayer.

◇ It begins, of course, with the very fact that thirty out of his thirty-three earthly years were spent in the relative silence and solitude of Nazareth.
◇ Just prior to beginning his public ministry, "Jesus, full of the Holy Spirit, then returned from the Jordan and was conducted by the Spirit, into the desert for forty days, where he was tempted by the devil." This was a time of fasting ("During that time he ate nothing") and presumably of intense praying (Luke 4:1–2).
◇ After his teaching and healing ministry started in earnest, Luke tells us, "he often retired to deserted places and prayed" (5:16)
◇ Before that momentous event of choosing the Twelve, only Luke records this detail: "Then he went out to the mountain to pray, spending the night in communion with God. At daybreak

he called his disciples and selected twelve of them to be his apostles . . . " (6:12).

◊ The transfiguration occurred in the context of prayer. "He took Peter, John and James, and went up onto a mountain to pray. While he was praying, his face changed in appearance and his clothes became dazzlingly white" (9:28–29).

◊ When Jesus gave us the Our Father and two parables on prayer, that teaching also occurred in a prayerful circumstance. "One day he was praying in a certain place. When he had finished, one of his disciples asked him, 'Lord, teach us to pray, as John taught his disciples.' He said to them, 'When you pray, say: Father, hallowed be your name, your kingdom come . . . ' " (11:1–2).

◊ As the conflict with the forces of darkness intensified during his last days, "he would teach in the temple by day, and leave the city to spend the night on the Mount of Olives. At daybreak all the people came to hear him in the temple" (21:37–38). Christ went from sunrise to sunset working, preaching and teaching, then prayed through the night.

◊ At Gethsemani we have the famous scene of his final prayer before the arrest. "In his anguish he prayed with all the greater intensity, and his sweat became like drops of blood falling to the ground." "An angel then appeared to him from heaven to strengthen him" (22:44, 43).

◊ Jesus' ultimate words on the cross formed a prayer taken from Psalm 31, verse 6: "Father, into your hands I commend my spirit" (23:46).

St. Paul preached about constant prayer and practiced it as well. From these excerpts out of Luke's Gospel, we can clearly see that the Apostle to the Gentiles was merely mirroring the teaching and modeling of his Master, Jesus. An examination of the other Gospels and of the entire New Testament reveals in further detail Christ's instruction on prayer and the Lord's own prayerful life.

Part III of this book contains the *General Instruction* to the *Liturgy of the Hours*, the Church's official prayer book. That document, in addition to explaining the content and mechanics of this

Liturgy of the Hours as we shall see later, also includes an extremely rich treatment on prayer. Articles 3–4 speak about "The Prayer of Christ" and summarize with over two dozen footnotes the scriptural picture we possess of Jesus as an example of prayerfulness. The running text alone deserves our reading; a more time-consuming examination of the footnotes and search for the references in the Bible will also prove very beneficial.

Such a study will remind us that the risen, glorified Lord continues to pray for those still in this world. "Jesus, because he remains forever, has a priesthood which does not pass away. Therefore he is always able to save those who approach God through him, since he forever lives to make intercession for them" (Hebrews 7:24–25).

Not surprisingly, contemporary disciples of Christ have imitated and do seek to follow Jesus' example of prayer.

The late Archbishop Fulton J. Sheen describes in his autobiography, *Treasure in Clay*, "The Hour That Makes My Day." At his ordination to the priesthood sixty years earlier, the famous preacher resolved to spend a continuous holy hour every day in the presence of Christ in the Blessed Sacrament. This particular chapter, "The Hour That Makes My Day," describes how he persevered in that resolution and what were some of the results. For example, it seems we as active people generally need a substantial period of time to quiet down and let the cares of our busy lives dissipate before we can enter into a deeper conversation with God. Archbishop Sheen writes:

> I have found that it takes some time to catch fire in prayer. This has been one of the advantages of the daily Hour. It is not so brief as to prevent the soul from collecting itself and shaking off the multitudinous distractions of the world. Sitting before the Presence is like a body exposing itself before the sun to absorb its rays. Silence in the Hour is a tête-à-tête with the Lord. In those moments, one does not so much pour out written prayers, but listening takes its place.[3]

Reverend David Wilkerson, a country preacher-pastor of a little mountain church in Philipsburg, Pennsylvania, regularly watched the Late Show on television for a couple of hours after his day's work. One night the movie seemed dull and lifeless, the story threadbare and shallow. He switched off the set, retired to his office, sat down in a brown leather swivel chair and pondered:

"How much time do I spend in front of that screen each night?" I wondered. "A couple of hours, at least. What would happen, Lord, if I sold that TV set and spent that time praying?" I was the only one in the family who ever watched TV anyway.

What would happen if I spent two hours every single night in prayer? It was an exhilarating idea. Substitute prayer for television, and see what happened.

Right away I thought of objections to the idea. I was tired at night. I needed the television and change of pace. Television was part of our culture; it wasn't good for a minister to be out of touch with what people were seeing and talking about.

I got up from my chair and turned out the lights and stood at my window looking out over the moonlit hills. Then I put another fleece before the Lord, one which was destined to change my life. I made it pretty hard on God, it seemed to me, because I really didn't want to give up television.[4]

Wilkerson made a deal with the Lord. He agreed to place an advertisement in the local paper for the television, and if a purchaser responded within half an hour, the preacher would sell the set and pray instead. The telephone rang twenty-nine minutes after the newspaper hit the stands. Wilkerson was now one television poorer, one hundred dollars richer and committed to a substantial period of prayer each day.

He describes the aftermath of that incident:

My life has not been the same since. Every night at midnight, instead of flipping some dials, I stepped into my office, closed the door, and began to pray. At first the time seemed to drag and I grew restless. Then I learned how to make systematic Bible-reading a part of my prayer life: I'd never before read the Bible through, including all the begats. And I learned how important it is to strike a balance between prayer of petition and prayer of praise. What a wonderful thing it is to spend a solid hour just being thankful. It throws all of life into a new perspective.[5]

Subsequently, Wilkerson followed an inner call to New York and began working with the big city's gang kids and developing "Teen Challenge," a movement to help "lost" boys and girls find themselves through finding God.

Mother Teresa is better known for picking up abandoned, dying lepers in the streets of Calcutta than for lecturing on the importance of prayer. She acknowledges, nevertheless, that the motivation behind these impressive charitable efforts is a recognition of Jesus' presence in every hurting individual. Moreover, the petite woman insists that without significant moments of prayer every day one cannot continue effectively to discover the Lord in the poorest of the poor. Mother Teresa's own community of women, the Missionaries of Charity, have as part of their daily regimen lengthy time for prayer in the morning and the evening.

We began this section with Father Henri Nouwen and conclude with him. In his book on desert spirituality and contemporary ministry, Nouwen argues for a set-aside time and place to be with God. He also records an exchange he had with Mother Teresa of Calcutta about his own prayer life and priesthood.

> The very first thing we need to do is set apart a time and a place to be with God and him alone. The concrete shape of this discipline of solitude will be different for each person depending on individual character, ministerial task, and milieu. But a real discipline never remains vague or general. It is as concrete and specific as daily life itself. When I visited Mother Teresa of Calcutta a few years ago and asked her how to live out my vocation as a priest, she simply said: "Spend one hour a day in adoration of your Lord and never do anything you know is wrong, and you will be all right." She might have said something else to a married person with young children and something else again to someone who lives in a larger community. But like all great disciples of Jesus, Mother Teresa affirmed again the truth that ministry can be fruitful only if it grows out of a direct and intimate encounter with our Lord.[6]

Spending a daily hour alone with God is a major step toward the goal of praying always, constantly and without interruption throughout the day.

Reflective Prayer Suggestions

1. Set aside five, ten or fifteen minutes for yourself alone, find a quiet place somewhere, read over Luke's account of Jesus' all-night prayer before selecting the Twelve (Luke 6:12–16) and then ask yourself: Do I regularly step apart by myself each day for a few moments of quiet prayer? If our Lord, with his busy life and important tasks, found time to do so, can I afford not to imitate Christ's example? Where, when and how should I accomplish this?

2. On another day, having found your few moments and quiet spot, read slowly the story of the ten lepers (Matthew 17:11–19) and, as Reverend David Wilkerson did, spend the rest of your prayer period being thankful to God for current big and small blessings you can recall.

3. Once you have begun a regular daily prayer routine or at least after you have experienced several periods of somewhat extended prayerful meditation, reflect back and see if you concur with the late Archbishop Sheen that it takes some time to catch fire in prayer.

◊ *Principle #2:*

Prayer is simply being present with God: Speaking and listening to the Lord in a variety of ways best suited for each individual.

> To you I pray, O Lord;
> at dawn you hear my voice;
> at dawn I bring my plea before you (Psalm 5:3–4).
> I will bless the Lord at all times;
> his praise shall be ever in my mouth (Psalm 34:2).
> I will give thanks to the Lord with all my heart
> in the company and assembly of the just (Psalm 111:1).
> Have mercy on me, O God, in your goodness;
> in the greatness of your compassion wipe out my guilt.
> Thoroughly wash me from my guilt
> and of my sin cleanse me (Psalm 51:3–4).
>
> The Lord called to Samuel, who answered; "Here I am." . . .
> The Lord came and revealed
> his presence, calling out as before, "Samuel, Samuel!"
> Samuel answered, "Speak, for your servant is
> listening" (1 Samuel 3:4, 10).

Principle #1 about prayer is essentially a matter of priorities. Do we judge some time alone with God each day to be an important value in our lives? If so, are we willing to take the practical step of experimenting to discover moments and places where we can regularly be present with the Lord?

Pastor John Killinger of the First Presbyterian Church in Lynchburg, Virginia views this priority decision to allocate specific time for prayer very much like the choice we make to spend some special period daily with a beloved friend.

17

Think of it this way. If there were someone you truly wanted
to get to know, to know in a very deep and meaningful way, you
would not consider it enough to visit with that person only in
the odd moments of your day. You would want to reserve a
time when you could sit down with him or her and be together
uninterruptedly as you talked and listened to one another. The
odd moments would be more valuable than ever in the light of
this period of concentration.[1]

This sounds eminently reasonable and easy enough, but most
readers know from experience that on-going responsibilities, un-
expected demands, frequent crises and the busy pressures of contemporary living make such a setting aside an often difficult
choice. It requires determination and discipline.

Persons doing so must also possess strong convictions that
these moments alone with God are not a selfish running away from
work, a careless abandonment of duty or a hurtful neglect of family. Given our American work ethic, the sometimes selfish de-
pendency of others upon us and one's conscientious attention to
the needs of those we care about, attaining this kind of certainty
may prove quite challenging. We can feel guilty or be told we
should feel guilty about taking this "wasted" time for prayer.
After all, are we not supposed to find Christ in our needing sister
or brother?

Prayer energizes us, and the few moments set aside each day
for explicit communion with God makes us better servants of others. That, however, may not be understood in the beginning by
those who object when we—on occasion—are no longer instantly
available for assistance. Still, as we persevere in the practice, its
impact on our lives and the deeper concern for family and friends
that it fosters within us will become apparent. In addition, the
very decision to find time and space for prayer and the carrying
out of this choice speaks to others about the importance of making
God a priority in our lives and, implicitly, in their own.

One workshop participant, a typically busy mother of six, discovered the difficulties and conflicts involved when she later applied this principle to her own life. Yet, in time the family seemed

to understand better and perhaps even to learn silently from her example. The woman wrote:

> Since listening to all your pointers on prayer I've started reading Scripture and saying the rosary. I have always tried to pray daily but now I feel I am concentrating better. It is still difficult at times in my home to find a quiet time and place to pray. I am the mother of six children (three boys and three girls). It seems no matter what time of the day or where I go to pray someone always needs me. They are getting better about leaving me alone now when I tell them I'm trying to pray.

As celibate priests, we have possibly better or easier control over the hours of our day than most lay persons, particularly those with family obligations. Nevertheless, we struggle with similar pressures, conflicts and even false guilt feelings about explicit time for prayer. The good priest has sometimes been identified as the busy priest. Time consequently set aside for communion with God can be seen, again, as wasted moments which make us less busy and thus less good.

The American Catholic bishops addressed that point in a booklet on "The Priest and Stress" by both naming the problem and suggesting the solution.

> One of the most probable causes of difficulties with spirituality in a priest's life today is simply his inability to find (or at least justify) sufficient time to spend in solitude and prayer. A conscientious priest, especially when under pressure of incessant demands, can forget that the quality of his work is more important than the quantity. What people are looking for in him more than anything else is a spiritual guide and model who will help them come to know the Lord and find His peace. Thus he must be, first of all and above everything else, a man of God's peace. Regular time each day for prayer, meditation, and spiritual reading is a *sine qua non* for the unfolding in a priest's life of an authentic Christ-centeredness.[2]

Once that first principle starts to be implemented on a regular basis and periods for prayer become a consistent priority as well as pattern of our lives, where do we go then? How do we actually use that space and time? What really is prayer?

This second principle offers an uncomplicated, but perhaps surprising definition of prayer: "It is simply being present with God: Speaking and listening to the Lord in a variety of ways."

John Killinger, cited above, no doubt would agree with that definition because he writes:

> Prayer is communion with God. It is the act of being with him. Nothing more, nothing less.
>
> It is coming into the presence of the One who loves us all the time—more than our parents ever loved us even in the best of times—and waiting in that presence.
>
> That's all. Coming and waiting.
>
> You pray in order to be with God.[3]

One of our workshop participants, a college student, found this explanation of prayer helpful. Trained to pray only with Our Fathers, Hail Marys or similar formulas, the collegian found such limitations unconsciously frustrating. A letter after the evening session summarized the difficulty and its potential resolution: "I remember mentioning to you about hoping to not rely so heavily on formal prayer and to learn to speak more freely and personally with the Lord. Well I still have some difficulty with that, but it's certainly easier than it was and I feel with practice and patience and prayer it will become yet easier."

Some will find this simple definition a pleasant surprise, either confirming what they have known all along or helping them realize that they pray more often and much better than they had judged.

A married person once expressed to me deep regret or even remorse about the absence of prayer in her life. "I hardly say any prayers at all." After only a few minutes' discussion, it became clear quite to the contrary that the woman prays daily and deeply. She takes a thirty to forty-five minute walk each day, and during the silence of that solitary jaunt speaks with God who is both present and communicates to her through the beauties of nature. The suggestion that she read a few lines of Scripture just before starting on the journey made practical sense for her and may help make that half hour or so of being present with the Lord even richer.

While our definition of prayer is surely uncomplicated and clear enough, it may prove valuable to offer a few recommendations about the place, the position and the preparation for praying.

Where Is the Best Place To Pray?

Jesus, as our model, answers that question. In the previous section we described how Christ prayed often and in various locations: deserted areas, mountainsides, synagogues, temples, upper rooms, gardens and, finally, on the cross. A disciple of the Lord, following his example, thus can pray in any place.

However, Christ's words in Matthew's Gospel about prayer, while adding another dimension to our title *Behind Closed Doors*, might seem, at first glance, to impose some restrictions in this regard.

> When you are praying, do not behave like the hypocrites who love to stand and pray in synagogues to be noticed. I give you my word, they are already repaid. Whenever you pray, go to your room, close your door, and pray to your Father in private. Then your Father, who sees what no man sees, will repay you (Matthew 6:5–6).

On the contrary, as Scripture scholars point out, Jesus here is not giving directions about where to pray, but instead condemning religious showiness through making an exaggerated statement. He and his disciples prayed often in public as all Jews did; they also retired to pray in private or alone. The Teacher consequently exaggerates—"go to your room, close your door, and pray to your Father in private"—to stress that we should avoid making a public display of ourselves in prayer and not seek to impress others. He in no way limits our locations for prayer.[4]

I personally find the church a most desirable place to pray for several reasons.

First of all, there tend to be no interruptions in church—no telephone calls, no visitors at the door, no questions from co-workers.

Second, a primary duty of the priest is to be a person of prayer. Although careful to observe Jesus' cautions about religious showiness just noted, we need also to follow Christ's dictate about letting our light shine before others. The clergy should be "for others" and generally available, but that does not mean at every moment of every hour in every day. It may be just as helpful for parishioners to see their pastor praying before the altar or hear that their priest "is over at church in prayer."

Third, an atmosphere of prayerfulness, awe and transcendence usually permeates the church building.

Finally, Catholic belief in the "real presence" of Christ under the signs of consecrated bread and wine adds a further benefit to the church as a place for prayer. Eucharistic adoration before the reserved sacrament in the tabernacle has been a gradual development in the Church and continues today to enjoy official support.

A recent Vatican document on the training of future priests was explicit and forceful on this point. Citing the extraordinary sanctity which has developed over the centuries from such prayer to and in the presence of the Eucharist, it goes on to remark:

> The number of whole communities specifically consecrated to this adoration are a guarantee of the authenticity of its inspiration. Someone like Brother Charles de Foucauld, alone in the desert with the Eucharist, yet shining out in the Church through his "little brothers" and "little sisters," is a most striking example of this in our own time. A priest who does not have this fervor, who does not acquire a taste for this adoration and is unable to communicate this to others is betraying the Eucharist itself and is blocking the way of the faithful to an incomparable treasure.[5]

Carlo Caretto, one of the Little Brothers of Charles de Foucauld, prepares for prayer outside, and then enters inside and prays before the tabernacle:

> Arising very early, a long time before daybreak, he goes out into the cold night air of the desert and sits on a hillside, watching the stars. He looks at the various constellations, and meditates on the grandeur of the One who created the heavens and the earth.
>
> Then he comes back into the small hermitage which Père de Foucauld built for himself, where the sanctuary lamp filled with olive oil flickers and casts its light on the earthen walls. Wrapping his *burnous* around him for warmth, he kneels down on the sand before the altar and begins to pray.
>
> Why doesn't he pray out on the hillside, under the stars?
>
> Because, says Brother Carlo, he prefers to come to God before the Eucharist, where God has given himself as bread.
>
> "It is here," he says, "that I have felt the presence of God most strongly; it is here that I have experienced for myself Christ's dramatic recapitulation of the history of salvation.
>
> "And I always come back here when I want to make my way to the threshold of the invisible, because the Eucharist is the surest doorway opening on to it."[6]

The hour which made Archbishop Sheen's day was a eucharistic period of adoration in the church before the altar. He made this faithfully throughout his priesthood and preached its value often to clergy, religious and laity alike. In his autobiography, Sheen describes the remarkable change such prayer before the Blessed Sacrament made in one man's life.

> Sometimes I wished that I had kept a record of the thousands of letters that I have received from priests and laity telling me how they have taken up the practice of the Holy Hour. Every retreat for priests that I ever gave had this as a practical resolution. Too often retreats are like health conferences. There is a general agreement on the need for health, but there is lacking a specific recommendation on how to be healthy. The Holy Hour became a challenge to the priests on retreat, and then

when the tapes of my retreats became available to the laity, it was edifying to read of those who responded to grace by watching an hour daily before the Lord. A monsignor who, because of a weakness for alcohol and consequent scandal, was told to leave his parish went into another diocese on a trial basis, where he made my retreat. Responding to the grace of the Lord, he gave up alcohol, was restored to effectiveness in his priesthood, made the Holy Hour every day and died in the Presence of the Blessed Sacrament.[7]

There is, nevertheless, no universally best place for prayer. It may be behind closed doors or with many people, in the tub or on the toilet, before the tabernacle or among rustling trees, in one's room or on an airplane.

Whenever we can find time could perhaps be the first determinant for a location. If we do have special moments available, however, then we should select the place where we are most relaxed, most comfortable, most able simply to be ourselves with and before God.

What Is the Best Position for Prayer?

Once again, there are no hard and fast rules here either.

However, we need not always be on our knees for prayer.

Reclining horizontally on the bed, couch or floor certainly is suitable, although that position may lead more to sleep than to prayer.

Generally speaking, for longer periods of reflective prayer or meditation the body will be most natural, comfortable and open to relaxation and refreshment "when the back is essentially straight . . . . For most of us in the West, a good chair that well supports the back offers the best opportunity for finding the right posture for . . . prayer."[8]

Moreover, we may use different postures for different types of prayer such as sitting while in meditation and kneeling while engaged in recitation of the rosary.

In summary, praying is the goal. Finding the best here and

now position for ourselves personally is but a means toward reaching that goal.

How Can We Best Prepare for Prayer?

In Part II under the section on meditation we will outline some very specific steps to help prepare mentally for the next day's reflective period. This will include reading of Scripture prior to retiring, selection of a word or phrase to aid in recalling the biblical passage, and use of that word or phrase during the final moments before sleep and immediately after rising.

Here, however, I wish to offer a few general comments and suggestions on how best to dispose our total being—body and spirit—for those various longer moments of prayer, particularly the ones which have a meditative character to them.

We do, of course, wish to cultivate the habit of frequently turning to the Lord during our waking hours. These are sort of momentary glances or a kind of conscious walking in God's presence as we move about our daily duties. But the lengthier, explicit sessions motivate us and facilitate such glances, walking or turning. Those can benefit from a few easy preparatory measures.

Selecting an *appropriate time* is one.

Some people are morning persons, others are night owls. My best moments, to illustrate, begin thirty minutes after rising and continue for the next six or seven hours; I go downhill after that. For me to meditate in the late evening would prove humanly quite unproductive. Others, on the contrary, never get their motors running in full gear until 10:00 a.m. or later. For such people late afternoon or even late night prayer sessions would be their best prayer times.

Normally for all, however, the hour following major meals will not lend itself to effective mental praying. Our heart, our blood, our body is working hard to digest the food we consumed; our life processes are centered on that project and the mind moves sluggishly until this task has been completed.

Nevertheless, praying at a particularly poor time is better than not praying at all.

Gently *closing our eyes* and keeping them closed is another practical measure. It has been estimated that we expend twenty-five percent of our psychic energy in seeing.[9] Lightly—not tightly—closing our eyes thus directs this energy inward rather than outward.

Before closing the eyes, however, some find it helpful to use a variety of *visual aids* for assistance in developing a prayerful atmosphere around and within them.

Jesuit Father George Maloney has done extensive research and writing on Eastern spirituality and about those prayerful monks of the desert who lived in the early centuries of Christianity. In his book *Prayer of the Heart*, Maloney supports in theory that practice of employing visual aids as a help with prayer and even suggests several specific ones:

> We are "whole" persons when we enter into prayer—persons of body, soul and spirit. It is only natural that material aids can help us to move from one level to another in a fuller integration of our total human nature in order to pray more completely as individuals meeting our unique, personalized God. We need signs and symbols drawn from our experiences in the world. Such signs are perceived as filled with spiritual meaning and they act on our consciousness, elevating it to a higher plane of awareness. Such signs as light, darkness, fire and breath have always found a special place both in communal and individual Christian prayer.
>
> We should not be in fear of such techniques if they truly do help us to pray better. Christians have always used them, and the hesychastic Fathers were in total agreement as they employed various aids in prayer.
>
> You can concentrate on a burning candle and be powerfully aware of Jesus Christ as the light of the world. A picture of a bubbling fountain can bring the words of Jesus to mind: "From his breast shall flow fountains of living water" (John 7:38). You can gaze lovingly at a tabernacle that contains the Blessed Sacrament, at a scene of nature, at an icon of Jesus Christ, Mary or the saints and find the calm that ushers you into a prayerful attitude. Music in church services has always been used as a calming and opening technique leading to prayerful worship.[10]

Finally, a *relaxation technique* or two can release our tensions and tightness, still the inner self and enable us to speak and listen to the Lord in a more calm, peaceful way.

Father Maloney notes that those ancient Christian mystics "learned that we all have to quiet our inner, psychic world, and this can be done easily by rhythmic breathing. The body, soul and spirit merge into a relaxed 'whole person' as God's breath is followed inwardly and outwardly, back and forth. . . ." "Just as athletes and singers, speakers and performers on stage seek to bring themselves to the maximum degree of concentration and relaxation by deep, rhythmical breathing, so we can learn from them how to sit quietly and breathe properly."[11]

Below are a few simple, easy to practice measures of relaxing our total self and putting our whole being into a proper condition for prayer. A period of prayer ought to prove restful and refreshing. These kinds of techniques can help in that regard, but they should be seen only as that—useful human exercises to facilitate our prayer. Use one, a few, all or none depending on your condition, needs and desires. These techniques are merely stepping stones to prayer and are to be measured for their value solely in terms of whether they help or hinder us in praying.[12]

◇ Sitting erect in a chair with hands extended on your knees, take a deep breath, hold it a moment, exhale and then gently close your eyes.

◇ Take another deep breath; hold it; be conscious of your inner feelings and exhale.

◇ Tighten up your entire body, clenching your fists in the process; hold for awhile and then gradually let go. Be aware in doing so of some tensions being released and disappearing.

◇ Drop your head on your chest for a moment or two, then slowly move it around to the left, tilting it back as you do so; then reverse the process to the right. Repeat the action. Be conscious of tight nerves untangling.

◇ Inhale deeply fresh oxygen and hold for a longer period of time, sensing the thoughts, emotions and images racing around inside you. Then exhale, releasing all those poisonous gases.

◇ Listen to your heart beat, pay attention to those pictures, feelings or ideas swirling within, and recall how you are a unique creation of God—no one is, has been or ever will be exactly like you. That specialness is especially apparent through the richness of your inner self.

◇ Tighten up once again your entire body, including the clenched fists; hold that pressure for a moment, then let go of the tenseness in your neck and allow it to descend to your back, down to your elbows, through your arms to your fists. Open your fists gently, slowly, and sense that tension pass through your fingers to your legs, down via the calves of your legs to your ankles, to your feet, through the soles of your feet into the ground and out. Be aware of how relaxed you are.

◇ Recall how Jesus said, "Anyone who loves me will be true to my word, and my Father will love him; we will come to him and make our dwelling place with him" (John 14:23). Thus, the Trinity, Father, Son and Spirit, is there, deep within you, down in the core of your being, bringing you peace.

◇ "Follow your breath down deeply within you, trying to relax as the flow of energy courses through your being, giving you new life and energy. When a basic rhythm of inhalation and exhalation has been established, seek to synchronize your breathing with the reverent repetition of the Jesus Prayer. As you breathe in, mentally say: 'Lord, Jesus Christ.' As you breathe out, say: 'Son of God.' Breathe in again as you say: 'Have mercy on me.' And, finally, breathe out with the words: 'A sinner.' "[13]

In conclusion, the reader should remember that prayer is speaking *and* listening to the Lord. Some explanations of the listening aspect will follow in subsequent sections. I need now, however, to note that since God does wish to speak with us on occasion we must be attentive to those signs which indicate this and be ready to hear the message that the Lord is apparently giving.

Reflective Prayer Suggestions

1. For a few successive days, use your prayer period to learn, experience and be comfortable with the relaxation technique just

outlined in this principle. Every month or so review those steps and practice them when preparing to pray.

2. Read over the excerpts from the four psalms at the start of this section and allow them to express or inspire within you sentiments and words of petition, praise or adoration, thanksgiving and contrition.

3. After reading either the excerpt about Samuel at the beginning of this chapter or all of Chapter 3 from 1 Samuel, spend the balance of your prayer time listening to God or at least remaining calm and in quiet waiting for the Lord to speak.

Different people will prefer different ways of praying and the same person may pray in several ways during a given day.

> There are different gifts but the same Spirit; there are differ-
> ent works but the same God who accomplishes all of them in
> everyone (1 Corinthians 12:4–6).

We mentioned at the outset of this section that there is no one way to pray, no model technique toward which we should strive, no perfect method in comparison with which all others are imperfect or found somehow wanting.

Prayer is simply being present with God, speaking and listening in the way most comfortable or productive for each one of us.

Our God is infinite, without limits. God's human creatures likewise share some of that limitlessness. Every individual has a uniqueness, a mysterious depth within never fully tapped. We are so varied and different that the diverse methods through which we reach the Lord and wait on him should come as no surprise.

We can pray *formally*, using words of others. Those phrases may come from the divine Scriptures like the Our Father or from human authors like the morning offering. Such formal prayers may be read or thought, recited or sung.

We can pray *informally* using our own words in a conversational or spontaneous way, such as in reflective meditation or thanksgiving after Communion. Such informal prayer may be done in the quiet of our hearts, for example, while having a cup of coffee in that locked bathroom, or spoken out loud, as during a charismatic prayer meeting.

We can pray *privately* or *individually* as we drive the car alone on the way to work.

We can pray *with others* or *communally*, such as at church for Sunday worship or in funeral homes during wake services.

We can pray *liturgically*, joining in the official prayer of the Church such as the Mass, the seven sacraments or the Liturgy of the Hours.

We can pray *non-liturgically*, employing prayers like the rosary or styles like meditation, all encouraged and approved by the Church, but not part of its official, liturgical worship.

Rev. John Killinger in his helpful book, *Prayer, the Act of Being with God*, after a few introductory sections on the attitude, time, place, posture and mood for prayer, gives over the rest of that text to twenty brief chapters, each one explaining a different way of praying. The mere listing below of the chapter titles should expand your own vision and show just how many methods are available and have been used to aid people commune with the Lord.

"The Prayer of Silence"
"Listening to God's Questions"
"Using a Single Phrase"
"The Jesus Prayer"
"The Use of Nonsense Syllables"
"Praying with a Mental Image"
"Fantasized Images"
"Praying Set Prayers"
"Meditating on the Scriptures"
"Fantasizing with the Scriptures"
"Meditating on Other Literature"
"Giving Thanks for All Things"
"Blessing Your Memories"
"Praying About Your Work"
"Praying About Your Dreams"
"Praying for Other Persons"
"Fantasized Scenes"
"An Imaginary Conversation with Christ"
"Subconscious Writing"
"Keeping a Prayer Journal"[1]

Killinger's list could be quite valuable for any person, beginner or veteran, seriously interested in prayer. Reading through those twenty chapters may create a desire to experiment with a few other or new methods of praying. Even in those people whose patterns of prayer have developed into a fixed comfortableness through years of repetition, such innovations could provide a fresh approach and perhaps renewed enthusiasm.

In Part II of this book we will explain at some length seven quite distinct methods commonly used by Roman Catholics. Those seven obviously do not exhaust the ways in which we pray. That section merely offers the reader practical steps for starting or enhancing some popular techniques of prayer.

This explanation in itself provided assistance to some of our workshop participants who recognized new possibilities for prayer in their busy lives. One woman wrote afterward: "As the mother of two small children whose prayerful moments are often limited to 'Grace Before Meals' and hearing bedtime prayers, your talk offered a few options I'm looking forward to exploring."

Many people seeking to become better disciples of Christ find they pray in a variety of ways on any given day.

My own prayer begins upon awakening with perhaps a sleepy attempt to recall some biblical phrase from the night before as I struggle to get out of bed. A mumbled morning offering on my knees follows, together with a Hail Mary. While shaving I try, more or less successfully, to remember again those scriptural texts I had selected for prayer the previous evening prior to sleep.

Then, normally, it is off to church for a few moments before the tabernacle of intimate, semi-spontaneous, getting started, early in the day remarks to the Lord in the Blessed Sacrament. The Liturgy of the Hours (Office of Reading and Morning Prayer) comes next, followed by about a half hour of meditation or centering prayer. This extended period of prayer in the morning, my best during the day, concludes with ten minutes or so of spiritual reading from Barclay's *The Daily Study Bible Series* and some other religious text.

I celebrate Mass either in the morning, at noon or in the late afternoon depending on local pastoral needs.

Recitation of the rosary usually comes while driving, a tough task with my stick shift car in city traffic, but relatively easy on longer trips over interstate highways. So far, in thirty years, I have had no accidents as a result of that praying while driving procedure.

Sometime during the day, normally upon return home after evening meetings or appointments, I finish the Liturgy of the Hours.

Throughout those waking and working hours I try to practice "constant prayer" or think of aspirations or be conscious of the Lord, but, regrettably, with uneven success. Intense mental preoccupation with my tasks at hand seems to block out any space for many such inner reflections.

There are occasional moments within the day of shared, spontaneous vocal prayer, sometimes before meetings, sometimes with an individual counselee.

Likewise my responsibilities may take me every now and then to a charismatic prayer session.

The day concludes with the Church's liturgical Night Prayer, reading of the scriptural texts for the next day's Mass, a brief on the knees prayer before climbing into bed, and then, while lying there, repetition of the biblical word, phrase or sentence selected for tomorrow's prayer. Since for me the interval between lying down and falling asleep usually can be measured in seconds, those final repetitious recollections are rather limited.

I have not related this account of prayer in a typical twenty-four hour period to impress readers—the Lord certainly knows my poverty both in prayer and virtue—but to illustrate the variety of methods used on one day by one person.

Following my workshop, I received this letter from an older woman, married, a mother, perhaps now a grandmother and also an office worker who similarly prays at different places and in different ways on the same day.

When I left the house that evening and told my husband where and why I was going, his parting words were, "What more could you possibly learn about praying that you don't already know?" It was only in jest that he spoke, but I pondered on that myself on the way to church.

While listening to you give the many ways of prayer, I realized I was already making use of the various methods. My day also begins with the morning offering, a throwback from my childhood days at St. Mary's in Rome. Daily Mass, whether it be early morning or sometimes evening, I try to go early enough for prayers and meditation. It takes me ten minutes to get to my office which is just time enough to pray the rosary. I have been offering up a decade for the four men in my life, my husband (who is not Catholic), and my three sons; two of whom are happily married and the third who is presently going for his Master's degree after completing four years with the Peace Corps in Paraguay. Since your workshop, I am now praying the rosary on the way home from work and offering up the decades for our priests, our sisters, the souls in purgatory, for the return of those who have left the Church and, selfishly, the last decade for myself, that God will continue to bestow on me his love and graces. Following dinner, I read from "God's Word Today" and often my husband will join with me in reading the passage from the Bible for the day as suggested. The day ends with my thanking God for giving me another day and I try to reflect on what good I had done or someone I have helped, and hopefully, God willing, I will wake to another day.

The Centering Prayer I found very relaxing and a nice time to just sit and think. Our prayer group leader initiated it at our session last Thursday and I'm sure we will be using that method in the future. My husband and I certainly know of the Prayer That Heals, for he was very near death two years ago and I know what it is to spend the night in prayer. We both know that the many prayers offered up for him brought him through.

We may pray in any way, at any time and in any place. But it should always flow out of and possess an essential element—faith. We will discuss that now.

Reflective Prayer Suggestions

1. Spend one prayer period reviewing the past week to discover how many different ways you ordinarily pray.

2. When you experience someone praying in a style quite different from your own, what do you think and how do you feel

about that? Do you make negative judgments concerning such a person or sense the presence of uncomfortable feelings within you? Or do you see there the Holy Spirit working in a rich variety of ways among a tremendous diversity of peoples, yet achieving the same goal—the praise and glory of an infinite God?

3. During a period of prayer, recall with gentleness and without strain the events of the previous twenty-four hours. As positive experiences, choices or deeds pass through your memory, give thanks to the Lord for such blessings and those opportunities to build up others, the Church and the world. When, on the contrary, certain negative experiences, choices or deeds enter your mind, simply ask God to help you grow through them and express your sincere repentance for the poor or selfish decisions you made.

◊ *Principle #4:*

Prayer is based on and builds up faith.

Do not let your hearts be troubled.
Have faith in God
and faith in me (John 14:1).

The massive dictionary on a stand next to my desk offers this as its initial definition of the word "faith":

The act or state of wholeheartedly and steadfastly believing in the existence, power, and benevolence of a supreme being, of having confidence in his providential care, and of being loyal to his will as revealed or believed in.[1]

That definition flows well from the Hebrew and Greek biblical words which serve as the root source for our terms "faith" and "to believe." Those ancient words convey the notion of firmness, solidity and constancy. They also communicate the concept of making oneself firm and secure, with this firmness and security based on God.[2]

We first encounter the word "faith" in the Bible during the story of Abram (later to be known as Abraham) in the fifteenth chapter of Genesis. That great patriarch had earlier at God's direction gathered his possessions and wife Sarah and left a comfortable homeland for the unknown land of Canaan. Now after a succession of events, the Lord came to Abram in a vision and promised him great rewards and gifts. Since he and Sarah were elderly and childless, Abram asked God how this could happen to a man without an heir.

The Lord then assured Abram he would have descendants as numerous as the stars in the sky. Because Abraham and Sarah "were old, advanced in years, and Sarah had stopped having her menstrual periods" (18:11), that prediction and promise of God staggered the imagination.

Nevertheless, we read that Abraham "put his faith in the Lord, who credited it to him as an act of righteousness" (15:6).

Abraham accepted the words God had spoken, surrendered his life to the Lord and loyally observed the Almighty's commands. In return for this act of faith, God carried out the divine part of that covenant or agreement as we discover in chapter 21, "The Lord took note of Sarah as he had said he would; he did for her as he had promised. Sarah became pregnant and bore Abraham a son in his old age, at the set time that God had stated" (21:1–2).

Abraham's example subsequently became a model of faith for all Christians.

St. Paul, writing to the Romans, spends the entire fourth chapter describing how Abraham was justified by faith. "For what does Scripture say? 'Abraham believed God, and it was credited to him as justice' " (4:3).

Paul wrote similarly to the Galatians in the third chapter about justification through faith and cites Abraham as a model to emulate. "Consider the case of Abraham: he 'believed God, and it was credited to him as justice.' This means that those who believe are sons of Abraham . . . thus it is that all who believe are blessed along with Abraham, the man of faith" (3:6–9).

The Church's worship reflects that biblical teaching about this Hebrew patriarch. It thus speaks in the first eucharistic prayer about "the sacrifice of Abraham, our father in faith."

We can discern three elements in Abraham's faith, ingredients which should be found in those like ourselves who claim to be daughters or sons of the patriarch.

There is an acceptance by the *mind* of words, ideas or truths spoken to us by the Lord. We believe in God's existence, power and promises; we believe in the Trinity; we believe in the Father's love, in Jesus' coming, dying and rising, in the Holy Spirit's outpouring on Pentecost and indwelling with us until the end of time; we believe in Christ's presence under the sign of bread and wine or oil and water, through the laying on of hands and the reading of Scripture, in the person who is hurting and the people with whom we worship. Our mind accepts, believes, has faith in these notions not because reason or logic tells us so, but because the all-truthful God revealed or taught them to us.

There is a surrender by the *heart*, a total inner reliance upon God's loving care for us, a complete turning of ourselves over to the Lord. We abdicate our own self-sufficiency and rely on God alone. We put our faith and place our trust in the Lord and in the Lord's promises to sustain and save us.

There is a carry-over into our *actions*, a conscientious application of God's directions to our own lives. Such external deeds are, as it were, proofs that we do accept these truths and have surrendered our lives over to the Lord. "So it is with faith that does nothing in practice. It is thoroughly lifeless. . . . Be assured, then, that faith without works is as dead as a body without breath" (James 2:17, 26).

The New Testament Epistle to the Hebrews contains a magnificent sketch of ancient Jewish leaders who displayed that kind of exemplary faith with this threefold dimension. After stating that the "just man will live by faith," and describing faith as "confident assurance concerning what we hope for, and conviction about things we do not see," the author notes, usually by name and always through deed, over a dozen persons who manifested such faith in their lives (10:38; 11:1–40).

"All of these died in faith," the writer comments. "They did not obtain what had been promised but saw and saluted it from afar. . . . The world was not worthy of them" (Hebrews 11:13, 38).

In the next chapter, however, the author takes the reader a step further and portrays Christ as the model for our faith. "Let us keep our eyes fixed on Jesus, who inspires and perfects our faith. For the sake of the joy which lay before him he endured the cross heedless of its shame. He has taken his seat at the right of the throne of God. . . . Remember your leaders who spoke the word of God to you; consider how their lives ended, and imitate their faith. Jesus Christ is the same yesterday, today, and forever" (Hebrews 12:2; 13:7–8).

Jesus not only modeled faith for us; he also frequently taught about faith.

◇ Christ praised, blessed and rewarded those who manifested faith in him, even making it a condition for many miracles that took place.

A Gentile, probably a pagan soldier, came to the Lord with his sick serving boy and humbly asked for a cure, confident that Christ could do it. "Jesus showed amazement on hearing this and remarked to his followers, 'I assure you, I have never found this much faith in Israel.' . . . To the centurion, Jesus said, 'Go home. It shall be done because you trusted.' That very moment the boy got better" (Matthew 8:5–13).

People brought a paralyzed man lying on his mat to Christ. "When Jesus saw their faith he said to the paralytic, 'Have courage, son, your sins are forgiven.'. . . 'Stand up! Roll up your mat, and go home.' The man stood up and went toward his home" (Matthew 9:1–8).

A woman who had suffered from hemorrhages for twelve years crept up behind Jesus and touched the tassel on his cloak. " 'If only I can touch his cloak,' she thought, 'I shall get well.' Jesus turned around and saw her and said, 'Courage, daughter. Your faith has restored you to health.' That very moment the woman got well" (Matthew 9:20–22).

Two blind men approached Christ crying out for his pity. "Jesus said to them 'Are you confident I can do this?' " When they replied affirmatively, he touched their eyes and said, " 'Because of your faith it shall be done to you'; and they recovered their sight" (Matthew 9:27–31).

One Canaanite woman pleaded with the Lord to cure her daughter terribly troubled by a demon. Reluctant to do so at the time because his ministry then was only to the Jews, the house of Israel, Christ finally succumbed to her ardent request. " 'Woman, you have great faith. Your wish will come to pass.' That very moment her daughter got better" (Matthew 15:21–28).

Thomas, who doubted at first, one week later made the famous act of faith, "My Lord and my God," as the risen Christ

showed him his hands and his side. Jesus then added: "You became a believer because you saw me. Blest are they who have not
seen and have believed" (John 20:24–29).

◊ Christ criticized, rather in a hurt way, and even chastized
those who displayed little or no faith.

In his often quoted exhortation about true riches and God's
providence, Jesus tells his hearers to stop worrying and adds, "If
God can clothe in such splendor the grass of the field, which
blooms today and is thrown on the fire tomorrow, will he not provide much more for you, O weak in faith" (Matthew 6:19–34; Luke
12:22–31).

When Christ and his disciples made their way across the Sea
of Galilee and a violent storm arose with the boat being swamped
by the waves, the frightened followers woke the soundly sleeping
Lord, crying out, " 'Lord, save us! We are lost!' " Jesus rebuked
them with, " 'Where is your courage? How little faith you have!'
Then he stood up and took the winds and the sea to task. Complete
calm ensued . . . " (Matthew 8:23–27).

Christ returned to his native place, Nazareth, and taught
there in the synagogue. Despite being amazed at his pronounce-
ments, "they found him altogether too much for them." This
prompted Jesus to observe, regretfully: "No prophet is without
honor except in his native place, indeed in his own house." Matthew concludes the episode by telling us, "And he did not work
many miracles there because of their lack of faith" (13:54–58).

In that great incident at which Jesus comes walking on the
waters during a middle of the night storm, he responds to Peter's
request and beckons the apostle likewise to walk on the water and
come to him. Peter does so for a few steps; then, perceiving how
strong the wind is, he becomes frightened, starts to sink and cries
out, " 'Lord, save me.' Jesus at once stretched out his hand and
caught him. 'How little faith you have!' he exclaimed. 'Why did
you falter?' Once they had climbed into the boat, the wind died
down" (Matthew 14:22–33).

After Jesus had cast a demon from the possessed boy, the disciples approached Christ privately and asked, " 'Why could we
not expel it?' 'Because you have so little trust,' he told them. 'I as-

sure you, if you had faith the size of a mustard seed, you would be able to say to this mountain, "Move from here to there," and it would move. Nothing would be impossible for you' " (Matthew 17:14–21).

At one discussion about bread and the yeast of the Pharisees and Sadducees, Jesus bluntly said, "How weak your faith is! Do you still not understand?" (Matthew 16:5–12).

◇ Christ predicted that the faith of his disciples would be tested or shaken.

During the Holy Thursday night events, Jesus said to his close followers: "Tonight your faith in me will be shaken, for Scripture has it: 'I will strike the shepherd and the sheep of the flock will be dispersed' " (Matthew 26:31).

◇ Christ promised great future blessings for those who possess and maintain faith.

Jesus promises eternal life on earth now for those who have faith. "Let me firmly assure you, he who believes has eternal life" (John 6:47). Through baptism and by sanctifying grace, we are lifted up and given a share in Christ's divine life already, here at the present moment, in this life. The Trinity dwells within us.

Jesus promises eternal life after our human death. "Indeed, this is the will of my Father, that everyone who looks upon the Son and believes in him shall have eternal life. Him I will raise up on the last day" (John 6:40).

Jesus promises that marvelous deeds will be performed by those who believe. "Signs like these will accompany those who have professed their faith: they will use my name to expel demons, they will speak entirely new languages, they will be able to handle serpents, they will be able to drink deadly poison without harm, and the sick upon whom they lay their hands will recover" (Mark 16:17–18).

Our Lord, then, praised, demanded, cautioned about and blessed faith. Some in his day, however, recognized the inadequacies of their own faith levels and pleaded with Christ for help in strengthening their faith.

The father of a possessed boy brought his son to Jesus requesting a cure. The Lord responded, " 'Everything is possible to a man who trusts.' The boy's father immediately exclaimed, 'I do believe. Help my lack of trust' " (Mark 9:14–29).

The apostles once simply said to the Lord, "Increase our faith" (Luke 17:5).

Two thousand years later people are making the same requests. "Help my lack of trust. I do believe. Increase my faith."

One young woman, for example, crushed by the tragic death of her brother in his early thirties, struggles to believe in heaven, to have faith in a world to come where that troubled man finally will find peace and where she will see him again. In prayer this lady asks God to bolster the fragile faith she possesses and which is being so sorely tested by that enormous grief engulfing her.

A much older woman waged a similar battle to believe in October 1978. However, the lady's struggle was not to find meaning in life after the death of a beloved, but to preserve faith in the face of her own imminent departure from this world.

The woman was Father Henri Nouwen's mother, and the priest describes his last moments with her through a moving book, *In Mei Memoriam.*[3]

He had received at Yale several days earlier a phone call from across the Atlantic indicating that his mother was near death in the Netherlands. Nouwen immediately flew from New York's JFK airport to Amsterdam and then made a two hour journey to the hospital where his mother, in pain, was entering upon the ultimate test of her faith.

Upon arrival the priest kissed his mother's forehead and touched her hand, then spent some time in a serene, gentle and prayer-filled reunion with this admirably devout Catholic Christian woman and the family. Afterward Father Nouwen left the hospital and went home for a few hours' rest.

When he returned in the evening her eyes had changed and her whole being reflected a shift in attention. She seemed, as it were, to have turned her concentration away from the family to the approaching encounter with God.

The woman dreaded that future meeting with the Lord. Three weeks earlier, Mrs. Nouwen had said to her son, "I am doubt, that great love reveals the possibility of hate and that great hope reveals the possibility of despair?[6]

He goes on to summarize his analysis of what was his mother's basic dread and why she felt that way: "It was this great encounter that frightened her. She was so deeply impressed by God's awesome greatness and had become so aware of her own nothingness that the great encounter could only frighten her."[7]

Nouwen expands in subsequent pages about that great chasm, gap or abyss between ourselves and God which only faith can bridge.

> It was the fear of the great abyss which separates God from us, a distance which can only be bridged by faith. The test comes when everything that is dear to us slips away—our home and those we love, our body and its many ways of living, our mind and its caring thoughts—and there is absolutely nothing left to hold on to. It is then that one must have the faith to surrender to a loving Lord, to believe that he will not allow us to fall into a cruel and bottomless canyon, but will bring us to the safe home which he had prepared for us. My mother knew her weaknesses and shortcomings. Her long life of deep prayer had not only revealed to her God's greatness, but also her own smallness; not only God's openheartedness, but also her own fearfulness; not only God's grace, but also her own sinfulness. It seemed that it was precisely her lifelong conversation with God that made her death such an agonizing event. At the hour of death all becomes faith. Faith in God, who knows every fiber of our being and loves us in spite of our sins, is the narrow gate which connects this world with the next.
>
> I saw my own mother entering into that moment in which we are totally alone with God, in which the final decision of life must be made: the decision of faith.[8]

From her depths during that ultimate struggle of faith, his mother cried out in prayer, "O God, my God, my Father, my God."[9] She was pleading for help to remain faithful, to persevere in belief that the Lord with tender love would eventually carry her over this enormous gulf between an imperfect creature and the perfect Maker.

afraid to die, not to go to the hospital, not to undergo surgery, not to suffer pain. I am afraid to appear before God and show him my life."[4]

We might expect that type of fear or dread from a person whose life had been marred by some serious moral failures or who had never regularly worshiped or for whom God seemingly had not been a very high priority. But this woman did not fit into any of those categories. On the contrary, the pattern of her spiritual life was most admirable, as her son testified when he wrote to his father after Mrs. Nouwen's death.

> You know better than I how important the Eucharist was for mother. There were few days in her adult life when she did not go to Mass and Communion. Although she did not speak much about it herself, we all knew that her daily participation in the Eucharist was at the center of her life. There were few things that remained so constant in her daily routine. Wherever she was or whatever she did, she always tried to find a nearby church to receive the gifts of Christ. Her great desire for this daily spiritual nourishment frequently led you to plan your trips in such a way that you both could attend Mass each day before resuming your travels.[5]

One hears often in connection with the death of an individual whose life appeared to be unusually virtuous, "Well if she (or he) doesn't make it to heaven, none of us has a very good chance!" Why, then, would such noticeably holy people like a Mrs. Nouwen fear or dread death because of the impending encounter with God?

After ministering the sacrament for the anointing of the sick to his mother, Nouwen pondered that issue and posed some questions to himself which suggest the answer:

> Could it be that I had applied oil on my own mother to help prepare her for the final battle? Is it not possible that she who lived her life in such close union with God had also come to know the power of the Evil One more intimately than many others? Is it inconceivable that she who had spent so many hours in prayer was also most aware of the one whom we call "the Tempter"? Is it not possible that great faith reveals the possibility of

At one point her son bent over and heard from her these words of prayer in which she continued to plead for faithfulness: "My Father who art in heaven, I believe, I hope, I love. . . . My God, my Father. . . ."[10]

But she did not pray alone for faith during those moments. Her son and family supported this woman with their own prayers. Nouwen recounts what happened at that time:

> I knew that this was the struggle of the great encounter. I wanted to give her the freedom she needed to enter into this lonely hour, to give her the space where this most mysterious of events could take place. I knew that she needed more than comforting words; she needed whatever support we could give her in this struggle of faith. With my father, brothers and sister, I prayed the prayers she hinted at—the Our Father, the Creed, the Hail Mary and the Litany of the Mother of God. In this way, we felt as if we offered her the words she could no longer speak herself, surrounding her with a shield of prayer that allowed her to fight her lonely battle.[11]

Praying that we remain faithful or grow in faith is not limited to death experiences, whether our own or others we care about.

A similar need arises whenever we are tested by trials, tempted to doubt or discouraged by sinfulness. At those moments we, like the dying woman, cry out that our faith may not falter.

For example, as we draw closer to God, our faith vision expands and sharpens, thus enabling us to grasp more clearly just how weak, sinful and limited we are and how awesome, holy and infinite God is. Here, too, faith alone can bridge this chasm, making us understand that the Lord wishes to heal and forgive us more than we often care to be healed and forgiven ourselves.

We pray to preserve and deepen our faith throughout such a difficulty confronting us.

Those prayerful petitions for an increase in faith lead us now to our next point—the relationship between prayer and faith.

Faith obviously is the basis or foundation for all prayer.

It is only because we believe with our minds those truths revealed to us in various ways by God that we pray at all. It is because we believe with our hearts that we in prayer cast our cares upon the Lord confident that God will sustain us. It is because we believe with our lives that we give ourselves over to different types of prayer such as Sunday worship or personal meditation.

Prayer, therefore, is an expression of our faith; it reflects our faith; it manifests our faith to others. But prayer also strengthens and deepens our faith.

In 1972 the American Catholic Bishops' Committee on the Liturgy issued a document, *Music in Catholic Worship*, which became a standard guideline for Church musicians. An introductory section of that text proposed a Theology of Celebration and summarized there rather nicely and powerfully these notions about the relationship between prayer and faith.

> We are Christians because through the Christian community we have met Jesus Christ, heard his word in invitation, and responded to him in faith. We gather at Mass that we may hear and express our faith again in this assembly and, by expressing it, renew and deepen it.
>
> We do not come to meet Christ as if he were absent from the rest of our lives. We come together to deepen our awareness of, and commitment to, the action of his Spirit in the whole of our lives at every moment. We come together to acknowledge the love of God poured out among us in the work of the Spirit, to stand in awe and praise.
>
> People in love make signs of love, not only to express their love but also to deepen it. Love never expressed dies. Christians' love for Christ and for one another and Christians' faith in Christ and in one another must be expressed in the signs and symbols of celebration or they will die.
>
> Faith grows when it is well expressed in celebration. Good celebrations foster and nourish faith. Poor celebrations may weaken and destroy it. [12]

Faith expressed in celebration is really one of the forms of prayer and, in fact, the most external, recognizable type of prayer. Those prayerful celebrations like all prayer have the power to nourish and foster our faith.

In these celebrations we do through faith meet Christ, as the document points out. Faith, in the definition of Bishop Frank J.

Harrison, is that which enables us to look beyond and recognize God's presence, to see beyond visible objects or events to the invisible Lord present through them. Faith thus empowers us to see or meet Christ; prayer is the context or setting in which that faith becomes active and allows us to perceive the risen Lord truly present in our midst.

We believe that God is present in many ways within and around us. This aspect of our faith has particularly rich ramifications for one's life of prayer. If we do truly grasp the multiple dimensions of Christ's presence, it can affect the manner in which we pray publicly or privately.

For example:

◇ I already noted under Principle #2 Jesus' promise: "Anyone who loves me will be true to my Word, and my Father will love him; we will come to him and make our dwelling place with him" (John 14:23). If we have faith in those words, then we need only turn within our hearts to speak with or listen to the Trinity.

◇ Paul wrote to the Romans: "We know that God makes all things work together for the good of those who have been called according to his decree" (8:28). If we have faith in that text, burdens in our lives, looked at in prayer, cease to be problems calling for solutions and become mysteries for us to experience.

◇ The Second Vatican Council fathers recognized the unique presence of Christ in the sacred liturgy. Paragraph 7 below, which enunciates that teaching, became the theological basis for all the subsequent worship reforms in the Roman Catholic Church.

> Christ is always present in his Church, especially in her liturgical celebrations. He is present in the Sacrifice of the Mass not only in the person of his minister, "the same now offering, through the ministry of priests, who formerly offered himself on the cross," but especially in the eucharistic species. By his power he is present in the sacraments so that when anybody baptizes it is really Christ himself who baptizes. He is present in his word since it is he himself who speaks when the holy Scriptures are read in the Church. Lastly, he is present when

the Church prays and sings, for he has promised "where two or three are gathered together in my name there am I in the midst of them" (Matthew 18:20). [13]

If we have faith in this doctrine about Jesus' multiple presence in the liturgy, it will affect the way we pray at Mass or before the tabernacle; it will influence our attitude when we receive or distribute the eucharistic species; it will deepen our awareness of what is happening when we celebrate any sacrament; it will raise our consciousness about the dignity of the scriptural word proclaimed in church or read at home; it will help us pray and sing better when we join others for communal worship.

◊ Psalm 8 begins, "O Lord, our Lord, how glorious is your name over all the earth!" It continues later, "When I behold your heavens, the work of your fingers, the moon and the stars which you set in place—what is man that you should be mindful of him; or the son of man that you should care for him?" (Psalm 8:2, 4–5). If we have faith in this biblical message, the wonders of God's creation become always available, ever changing stepping stones for a prayer of gratitude and praise.

Prayer flows out of faith, but it can also bring faith into a person's heart. Our prayer finds its basis and inspiration in faith, but prayer likewise fosters and nourishes faith.

Reflective Prayer Suggestions

1. Read rather slowly chapter 11 of the Letter to the Hebrews and catch the numerous examples of a faith which looked beyond the here and now to the promised yet to come and in so doing spurred many believers on to heroic acts.

2. When you have a few minutes of quiet time, settle yourself, read the story about a possessed boy in Mark 9:14–29 and ask the Lord to increase your faith, especially in times of stress that test your trust in God.

3. Reflect on how alive is your faith in Christ's many presences among us and how much that belief affects your acting, speaking, thinking and praying. To help this reflection process, refresh your memory about those various ways God is present described in the last part of this section.

Prayer, like faith, may overflow into our feelings, but not necessarily.

They went then to a place named Gethsemani. "Sit down here while I pray . . . ." Then he began to be filled with fear and distress. He said to them, "My heart is filled with sorrow to the point of death . . . ." He advanced a little and fell to the ground, praying that if it were possible this hour might pass him by.

An angel then appeared to him from heaven to strengthen him. In his anguish he prayed with all the greater intensity, and his sweat became like drops of blood falling to the ground (Mark 14:32–35; Luke 22:43).

I remember hearing years ago a story about some young student for the priesthood who experienced in the seminary quite different reactions during two sessions of prayer.

One sunny afternoon he paused to pray in the chapel for an extended time. All there was still and peaceful; the light shining through stained glass windows created a remarkable environment; this future priest had slept long and soundly the night before; that day's classes together with other events seemed to have gone extremely well.

His prayer on this particular afternoon also flowed along quite smoothly. He felt close to God, prayed easily, hardly noticed the time slipping by and left the church on an emotional high.

Since that interval of prayer had produced such wonderful feelings within him, the next day he sought to repeat the experience. Same time, same place, same format.

Yet nothing happened. He didn't feel particularly elated; the time dragged along. His mind moved distractedly from one thought to another; and he left the chapel rather downcast.

This incident and the seminarian's naiveté may amuse us, but it does highlight the fluctuating nature of our feelings. We pray one day and feel near the Lord; we pray on another and God seems distant or aloof. It also underscores the principle that prayer may overflow into our feelings, but not necessarily.

Feelings, by their nature, are quite ephemeral. They come and go, ebb and flow, often without rhyme or reason.

Over the past decade I have been closely associated with many persons and groups touched by the emotions connected with dying, death and bereavement. What has particularly struck me is the wave-like nature of feelings in the grief process. The mourning individual normally senses the beginning of sadness in the stomach, feels it climb to the top of the head and, there, overwhelm or engulf the person. But after some moments the intense feelings tend to subside, retreat from the head, eyes or throat and disappear, leaving the individual still saddened but less agitated and distraught.

This ebb and flow, wave-like characteristic parallels the experience of swimmers in the ocean or a large lake. They may be standing quite comfortably at one moment in several feet of water and the next minute be swallowed up by a massive wave. Veterans to this phenomenon adjust nicely to it. These people calmly dive through, float with or wait for the wall of water to subside, knowing that shortly they will surface and be able to breathe again, with the ocean or lake back at its lower level until the next wave.

Beginning swimmers or strangers to such ocean bathing may not react so easily. Inexperienced, they may stiffen and fight the waves, finding themselves roughly thrown to the bottom in the process. Or, fearing that they have been buried by the waters, will not come to the top for air naturally and are thus in danger of drowning, they may frantically flail about seeking the surface.

People engulfed in grief, or any other similar down feeling, occasionally react much like those beginning swimmers or unfamiliar ocean-goers. They may try to fight the emotion itself or wildly and often falsely flee for some way, someone, something to dispel the unpleasant feeling.

An awareness of the undulating nature of our emotional life can help us keep our balance during such low moments.

Jeanne McNamara, a woman in her sixties, will attest to that. One Sunday morning she learned by telephone that her brilliant, thirty-eight year old lawyer-son had been knifed to death during a senseless mugging attack the night before in New York City. That afternoon as she sat at home speechless, staring ahead with a stolid and dazed expression on her face, a clergyman offering comfort explained briefly the wave-like nature of grief feelings. The woman hardly reacted to his words, but a half hour later she whispered, "I am feeling one of those waves." That understanding helped Jeanne in subsequent days to cope with this terrible tragedy and her enormous sense of loss.

Such an awareness can likewise help us keep a proper perspective in our prayer life. Like the seminarian, we may have days when we feel elated at or after prayer and other occasions when we feel dry or downcast during or following a period of prayer. Neither should be seen as an accurate criterion of how well or poorly we have prayed or how close or distant we are to God.

A partial cause of the difficulty in maintaining that clear distinction between faith and feelings is the erroneous understanding of the term celebration as applied to liturgy which has developed in recent years.

Long before the Second Vatican Council the Church consistently spoke of liturgical worship or public prayer as a celebration. Thus, the Latin term for offering the Eucharist was "celebrare Missam"—"to celebrate Mass"; a priest was known as the celebrant; many seminarians in learning how to function at the altar followed a text entitled *The Celebration of Mass* by O'Connell.

After the Council, the restored ritual books continued to employ the same term. For example, the initial chapter in the General Instruction on the Roman Missal is called "Importance and Dignity of the Eucharistic Celebration," and the word "celebration" occurs ten times in the six short paragraphs of that chapter.

Celebration, then, is not a new word or concept. However, it began to assume for some a different meaning during the liturgical changes of the post-Vatican II era. Wishing to stress the joyful, communal, victorious, participatory and musical elements of worship, these leaders took the ingredients of human celebrations like a birthday party, wedding reception or anniversary commemoration and applied them without modification to the liturgy.

Since most participants at these secular events generally experience some kind of uplift in feelings, often stimulated by refreshments, it was consequently judged that good liturgical celebrations should have the same tone and produce similar effects. We ought to feel good about going to Mass, feel good during the liturgy and feel good afterward. We should get something out of worship and a "whoopee" atmosphere in liturgy would not be totally out of place.

The problem here is that sometimes members of the community at public prayer do experience such an emotional uplift and at other times for a variety of reasons do not. According to the human celebration criterion, the latter liturgies therefore failed in some way either for the entire body or at least for those individuals not particularly moved on the feeling level by them.

Two examples may help clarify this point.

Several Easters ago at Most Holy Rosary Church in Syracuse, the liturgy committee mimeographed copies of a short paschal greeting and inserted these into 750 balloons. They then inflated the balloons with helium and after the 9:45 children's liturgy handed them to departing worshipers who walked across the street and assembled in a public park.

At a given signal the many, multi-colored balloons drifted upward, marvelous symbols of rejoicing and faith in the resurrection. Later in the week two persons wrote from several hundred miles away expressing their happiness at the discovery of a balloon with its message inside and communicating their own best wishes to the parishioners at the Syracuse church.

The priest leader, in recounting the event, commented, "That was a real celebration."

I agree. However, I also am a bit uneasy with the implication that this was a "real celebration" simply because of the joy and enthusiasm which accompanied it. For, if that is our measuring rod, then we could not judge or label Betsy O'Shea's funeral Mass a true celebration.

On a Sunday morning, also several years ago, the feast of the Holy Family, Betsy never woke up. Her husband Jerry heard murmurs during sleep that night and thought his thirty year old wife must have been going through a nightmare. The young woman, a registered nurse working part-time at the local hospital and mother of three children, had never been ill before.

Betsy's sudden death naturally shocked all and devastated her husband.

A thousand friends crowded Holy Family Church for the Mass of Christian Burial. They wept with and for the husband, especially as Jerry carried the oldest child, Kathleen, age 4½, in his arms as he moved forward to receive Communion. But they also heard words and experienced symbols of hope and resurrection.

Was this not also a "real celebration"?

We judge both to have been true, authentic celebrations because in each one we celebrated in faith the victory of Jesus over death. In the first, the Easter event, that faith overflowed into feelings and sent people away quite joyous, excited and happy. In the second, Betsy's funeral, that faith also may have spilled over into feelings, but not necessarily, and, if so, in a distinctly different way.

If we equate faith and feelings, prayer and feelings, worship and feelings, we doom ourselves to frequent frustration and ultimate doubts. If we grasp the close but not necessary connection between faith, prayer, worship and feelings, we will move forward on life's journey with greater calmness and clearer direction.

The American Bishops' Committee on the Liturgy in its document *Music in Catholic Worship* simply and succinctly summarized this issue of the relationship between faith and feelings:

> Celebrations need not fail, even on a particular Sunday when our feelings do not match the invitation of Christ and his Church to worship. Faith does not always permeate our feelings. But the signs and symbols of worship can give bodily expression to faith as we celebrate. Our own faith is stimulated. We become one with others whose faith is similarly ex-

pressed. We rise above our own feelings to respond to God in prayer.

Having said that, the bishops also went on to state that those who plan and carry out liturgies should make them as humanly attractive as possible. Unless they are meaningful and appealing to the body of worshipers, these rites "will fail to stir up faith and people will fail to worship the Father."

There is a very practical conclusion to this discussion on prayer and feelings: the desired goal of having a determined period for prayer each day.

Some of those workshop participants asked for guidance from me on how much time they should allocate for that daily prayer session. My response has been to stress the consistency of this prayer period, day after day whenever possible, rather than its length. That will help insure that we pray both when we feel like communicating with the Lord and when we are not particularly in a mood to do so.

Nevertheless, establishing a rather definite, although flexible, length of time available and comfortable for us also possesses value. It will keep us praying on those dry dark days when we may be tempted to cut short our set-aside visit with God. It may also prompt us to terminate our explicit prayer on rich, uplifting days when we might enjoy tarrying in the Lord's presence, but really must be about our other duties.

Reflective Prayer Suggestions

1. Read over one or all three accounts of Jesus in Gethsemani (Matthew 26:36–46; Mark 14:32–42; Luke 22:39–46) and ponder how Christ prayed even though he felt great sadness and did not receive the request he first sought.

2. Recall a relatively recent loss in your life and try to remember or even relive the wave-like nature of feelings you experienced. Or reflect on current times you have prayed and the

positive, negative or empty feelings which accompanied those periods of prayer.

3. Determine what would be a good length of time for you to set aside for prayer, stick to it for a week and evaluate the up and down feelings you experienced as you prayed during those seven days.

Any regularly praying person can expect moments and periods of purifying dryness and darkness.

There is cause for rejoicing here. You may for a time have to suffer the distress of many trials; but this is so that your faith, which is more precious than the passing splendor of fire-tried gold, may by its genuineness lead to praise, glory and honor when Jesus Christ appears (1 Peter 1:6–7).

The very ephemeral nature of our emotions—their temporary presence and fluctuating character—means that our prayer life must be rooted in faith and not based upon feelings.

If we feel happy and devout at prayer, that makes our praying easier and more humanly satisfying. This should prompt inner sentiments and acts of gratitude to the Lord. If, on the other hand, we feel burdened and dry, that makes our praying harder and less naturally gratifying. But it ought not to trouble us or cause us to worry about our status before God. Instead we need merely to continue our prayer with calmness, perseverance and faith.

In addition to the transitory nature of feelings, there are two other reasons why we cannot expect periods of prayer always to be filled with uplifting, positive and comforting emotions: the pattern of Christian life promised by Jesus and the stages of the interior life described by the classical spiritual masters.

◊ First, the pattern of Christian life promised by Jesus.

In each of the Synoptic Gospels of Matthew, Mark and Luke we can note a triple prophecy of Christ's paschal, passover or Easter mystery. Three times Jesus predicts he will go up to Jerusalem, be rejected, suffer greatly and die there, then be raised up on the third day. But before every prophecy we read about a miracle our Lord performed, and after each prediction the Savior teaches that his followers must also undergo in various ways their own death and resurrection experiences.

Thus, according to Matthew's account, Jesus utters his first prophecy of the passion and resurrection in chapter 16:21–23. Immediately before we read how Christ miraculously fed four thousand with seven loaves and a few small fish (15:32–38). Immediately after the passion prediction, our Lord teaches his doctrine of the cross: "If a man wishes to come after me, he must deny his very self, take up his cross, and begin to follow in my footsteps. Whoever would save his life will lose it, but whoever loses his life for my sake will find it" (Matthew 16:24–25). Luke's version includes this additional element, "take up his cross each day" (Luke 9:23).

The second prophecy, in Matthew 17:22–23, repeats that earlier message: "The Son of Man is going to be delivered into the hands of men who will put him to death, and he will be raised up on the third day. At these words they were overwhelmed with grief."

It, too, was preceded by a miracle, the transfiguration of Jesus on the mountain (Matthew 17:1–8) and followed by a practical application of the passion-resurrection prediction to his followers: "Just then the disciples came up to Jesus with the question, 'Who is of greatest importance in the kingdom of God?' He called a little child over and stood him in their midst and said: 'I assure you, unless you change and become like little children, you will not enter the kingdom of God. Whoever makes himself lowly, becoming like this child, is of greatest importance in that heavenly reign' " (Matthew 18:1–4).

Our Lord's warning against ambition in effect served as a concrete adaptation of the paschal mystery to the lives of Christ's followers.

The third and final prophecy (Matthew 20:17–19) has this preceding event; "Great crowds followed him and he cured them there" (Matthew 19:2). It likewise is followed by a practical application, in this case an instruction of Jesus prompted by the mother of Zebedee's request for honors for her sons: "You know how those who exercise authority among the Gentiles lord it over them; their great ones make their importance felt. It cannot be like that with you. Anyone among you who aspires to greatness must serve the rest, and whoever wants to rank first among you must serve the needs of all. Such is the case with the Son of Man who has come, not to be served by others, but to serve, to give his own life as a ransom for the many" (Matthew 20:20–28).

These doctrines of the daily cross in a Christian's life, the importance of rooting out ambition and the call to become servants even to the point of dying for others should lead us to expect some crosses, humiliations and deaths in our prayer periods.

◊ Second, the stages of the interior life described by the classical spiritual masters.

When we check the writings of such authors in any era of Church history, this common theme or element regularly appears: those who seriously seek union with God must expect some type of persecution, tribulation or purification.

For example, St. Paul in the first Christian century preached that notion. St. Thomas Aquinas in the thirteenth taught the same concept. St. John of the Cross, St. Teresa of Avila and St. Francis de Sales in the sixteenth century all maintained a similar position. Jesuit Father George Maloney likewise upholds this principle in our own day.

Perhaps the clearest and best known exposition of the part that purifications play in our prayer life and our path to perfection comes from the pen of St. John of the Cross, the Spanish mystic who lived 1543–91.

This master maintained that both the full perfection of Christian life and a contemplative form of prayer are accessible to any person truly intent on walking in Jesus' footsteps and are not restricted to a few exceptional individuals.[1]

To achieve those goals of perfection and contemplation which are considered preludes here to the joyful union and face-to-face vision of God in heaven hereafter, St. John of the Cross declares that the person must undergo a passive purification of the senses and a subsequent passive purification of the spirit.[2]

According to his schema, there are three ages of the interior life—the purgative period of beginners, the illuminative phase of proficients and the unitive stage of the perfect. In between the purgative and illuminative phases stands the passive purification of the senses; between the illuminative and unitive occurs the passive purification of the spirit.[3]

While agreeing that we must do our own part to grow in holiness through self-imposed ascetical practices of penance and mortification, St. John of the Cross teaches that another cleansing, a passive purification, a purgation from outside is also necessary for perfection and contemplation.

In his words, "For, after all the efforts of the soul, it cannot by any exertion of its own actively purify itself so as to be in the slightest degree fit for the divine union of perfection in the love of God, if God Himself does not take it into His own hands, and purify it in the fire, dark to the soul, in the way I am going to explain."[4]

Father Garrigou-Lagrange, in a massive two volume study on *The Three Ages of the Interior Life*, puts in his own words the teaching of St. John of the Cross on that dark night or *passive purification of the senses* which persons serious about prayer and the Christian life encounter as they move out of the beginning stage of spirituality into a more advanced and proficient level.

> First of all, the soul is weaned from sensible consolations, which are useful for a time but become an obstacle when sought for themselves. Whence the necessity of the passive purification of the senses, which places the soul in sensible aridity and leads it to a spiritual life that is much more freed from the senses, the imagination, and reasoning. At this point the soul receives, through the gifts of the Holy Ghost, an intuitive knowledge which, despite a painful obscurity, initiates the soul profoundly into the things of God. At times this knowledge makes us penetrate them more deeply in an instant than would meditation over a period of months and years. To resist temptations against chastity or patience—temptations which present themselves rather frequently in this night of the senses—there are required at times heroic acts of chastity and patience, which are, however, extremely fruitful.
>
> In the night of the senses there is a striking light and

shade. The sensible appetites are cast into obscurity and dryness by the disappearance of sensible graces on which the soul dwelt with an egotistical complacency. But in the midst of this obscurity, the higher faculties begin to be illumined by the light of life, which goes beyond reasoned meditation and leads to a loving and prolonged gaze upon God during prayer.[5]

That dark night of the senses, painful as it may be, does cleanse the heart. If every prayer of ours brings us consolations or good feelings, there is a danger that we may begin praying more for the consolations of God than to the God of all consolations. The removal for a time of such comforting and satisfying emotions helps keep our motivation pure and our vision in proper perspective. It liberates us from excessive attachment to the creatures of God and enables us to love more fervently and with greater single-mindedness the God of all creation.

But this purification of the senses also works at eliminating within us certain sins and evil inclinations. Garrigou-Lagrange develops that point in detail:

> Not without suffering indeed is complete victory obtained over egoism, sensuality, laziness, impatience, jealousy, envy, injustice in judgment, self-love, foolish pretensions, and also self-seeking in piety, the immoderate desire of consolations, intellectual and spiritual pride, all that is opposed to the spirit of faith and to confidence in God, that a man may succeed in loving the Lord perfectly, with his whole heart, with his whole soul, with all his strength, and with all his mind, and his neighbor (enemies included) as himself. Great firmness, patience, and longanimity are also needed to persevere in charity, whatever may happen, when the words of the apostle are verified: "And all that will live godly in Christ Jesus shall suffer persecution."[6]

The regularly praying person who has moved out of the beginner's stage, weathered well the dark night of the senses, and moved into the plateau of proficients eventually must experience a deeper, more painful *passive purification of the spirit*. Garrigou-Lagrange likewise discusses at length the why, the what and the result of that dark night of the spirit.

But even after this purification, that the soul may be freed from the defects of proficients, from the subtle pride which subsists in them, another purification, that of the spirit, is needed. This purification is found in far more advanced souls which ardently desire goodness, but which have too strong a desire that good be done by them or in their way. They must be purified from every human attachment to their judgment, to their excessively personal manner of seeing, willing, acting, from every human attachment to the good works to which they devote themselves. This purification, if well borne in the midst of temptations against the three theological virtues, will increase tenfold their faith, their confidence in God, and their love of God and neighbor.

This purifying trial presents itself under rather varied forms in the purely contemplative life and in that devoted to the apostolate. It differs also according as it is intended to lead the soul even here on earth to lofty perfection, or when it occurs only at the end of life to help souls to undergo, at least partially, their purgatory before death while meriting, while growing in love, instead of undergoing it after death without meriting. The dogma of purgatory thus confirms the necessity of these passive purifications of the senses and of the spirit.

In this trial there is a light and shade superior to that of the night of the senses. The soul seems stripped of the lights and the facility to pray and to act in which it took satisfaction because of a remnant of self-love and pride. But a superior light appears in this night of the spirit; in the midst of temptations against faith and hope appear little by little in all their relief the formal motives of the three theological virtues. They are like three stars of first magnitude: the first revealing truth, the helpful mercy, and the sovereign goodness of God. The soul comes to love God very purely with its whole heart; it becomes an adorer in spirit and in truth.[7]

This concept of two passive purifications merely puts into practical, specific terms the more theoretical, generic promise or admonition of Jesus. "I am the true vine and my Father is the vine grower. He prunes away every barren branch, but the fruitful ones he trims clean to increase their yield" (John 15:1).

St. Thomas Aquinas, the great teaching Doctor of the Church

in the Middle Ages (1225–1274), has this commentary on that passage which links it with the dark nights of the sense and spirit described above:

> In the life of nature it happens that a palm tree having many sprouts bears less fruit because of the diffusion of the sap to all the branches. Thus, in order that it may bear more fruit, cultivators trim away its superfluous shoots. So it is in man. Now, if in a man who is well disposed and united to God, his affection inclines to diverse things, his virtue decreases and he becomes more ineffective in doing good. And so it is that God, that the man may bring forth fruit, frequently cuts away impediments of this type and purges him, sending tribulations and temptations by which he may be made stronger for action. Therefore He says: "He will purge him," even if he is pure, because nobody is so pure in this life that he cannot be more and more purified.[8]

Those two reasons, then, the pattern of Christian life promised by Jesus and the stages of the interior life sketched by classical spiritual writers, plus the very transitory nature of feelings, lead us to this chapter's principle: "Any regularly praying person can expect moments and periods of purifying dryness and darkness."

Perseverance in prayer during such purifying periods, always a challenge, can be particularly difficult in the climate of our contemporary society.

Daniel Yankelovich, a respected analyst of social trends and public attitudes, in his book *New Rules: Searching for Self-Fulfillment in a World Turned Upside Down*, has summarized extensive research on the recent change in Americans' attitudes toward self-denial and self-fulfillment.

Prior to the 1970's, most citizens in this country espoused a self-denial ethic or philosophy of life. They were quite willing to postpone their immediate desires or wants for longer term goals. These sought after ideals generally centered around worldly or family success.[9]

Thus, the breadwinner held two jobs or both spouses worked. Moreover, these people sacrificed certain pleasures they would have enjoyed, saved money, accepted painful transfers for the sake of a rise in the corporation ladder and normally did everything possible to insure a secure and comfortable financial future. In addition, spouses, although disenchanted with each other, stayed together for the sake of the children, and parents often gave up their own pleasures so that their offspring might prosper.

It was, in Yankelovich's terminology, a "giving/getting compact," with giving normally now and the getting usually later. He paraphrases that attitude in this way:

> "I give hard work, loyalty and steadfastness. I swallow my frustrations and suppress my impulse to do what I enjoy, and do what is expected of me instead. I do not put myself first; I put the needs of others ahead of my own. I give a lot, but what I get in return is worth it. I receive an ever-growing standard of living, and a family life with a devoted spouse and decent kids. Our children will take care of us in our old age if we really need it, which thank goodness we will not. I have a nice home, a good job, the respect of my friends and neighbors; a sense of accomplishment at having made something of my life . . . ."[10]

The key words of that paraphrase, in my judgment, are hard work, loyalty, steadfastness, swallowing frustrations, suppressing impulses for immediate pleasure or enjoyment, fulfilling responsibilities or expectations, putting self last and others first. All of these suggest a truly self-denial ethic.

But in the 1970's a radical shift took place among Americans. All national surveys indicated an increase in preoccupation with self. Yankelovich's own studies revealed that seventy-two percent of Americans were spending a great deal of time thinking about themselves and their inner lives. That trend amounted, in his terms, to a virtual "rage for self-fulfillment."[11]

This meant that the old self-denial rules and the acceptance of deferred gratification had lost their normative power. "No moral virtue is attached any longer to the idea that it is good to curb the imperatives of the self. Under the old ethic, self-denial was assumed to have virtue for its own sake; under the self-fulfillment ethic self-denial makes no sense."[12]

In such a shift people tend to be "forever preoccupied with

their inner psychological needs. They operate on the premise that emotional cravings are sacred objects and that it is a crime against nature to harbor an unfulfilled emotional need."[13]

If Yankelovich's findings and conclusions are accurate, then it should be obvious that persevering in prayer when our inner selves seem dry and dark goes contrary to the current attitude or ethic. Struggling with courage and faith through the passive purification or dark night of sense or spirit hardly satisfies our "emotional cravings" or "unfulfilled emotional needs." On the other hand, constancy in prayer, when we seem to be deriving little surface, human or emotional satisfaction, does require considerable discipline and self-denial, a hope-filled but deferred gratification of desires.

It should be noted that these are generalizations, that the turn of Americans inward can and has led many to prayer and that there is a deep spiritual contentment which arises when one dies to self through perseverance in prayer during dryness and darkness. Still, our self-fulfillment culture does influence us and we are inclined as a result to give up a responsibility, project or relationship when encountering obstacles.

Damien de Veuster (1840–1889) lived long before that current shift to the self-fulfillment ethic and away from the self-denial approach of former years. In fact, his whole life, especially the last two decades of it spent caring for the lepers of Molokai, modeled the self-giving service of others ideal that Jesus preached. Yet he, too, experienced a passive purification of body and spirit in the latter years of his ministry on that Hawaiian island.

At some unidentifiable point during his work with the lepers, the Belgium-born priest contracted the disease itself. Little by little that dreaded affliction crippled his body leaving him disfigured, in pain and weak.

Difficult as was the physical ailment, Father Damien suffered more from loneliness, rejection by superiors and worry about his own spiritual condition. Nevertheless, he sought in prayer light and courage to endure the trial. Damien wrote:

> I resign myself to Divine Providence, and find my consolation
> in the only companion who does not leave me—that is to say,

our Divine Saviour in the Holy Eucharist; it is at the foot of the altar that I often confess myself and seek relief from spiritual pain.[14]

He had requested permission from the authorities of his religious community to visit occasionally another island, Oahu, and there in Honolulu to receive any treatment for the disease available and to make a sacramental confession.

They refused his petition. That refusal and the way it was handled caused "a sort of blackness" to come over Damien and he began to think of his village on Molokai as a "tomb."[15] Wounded by their decision and the sharp, accompanying comments, Damien wrote that "this absolute refusal, expressed in the voice of a policeman rather than a religious superior, and in the name of the bishop and the prime minister, as if the mission would be quarantined if ever I showed myself at Honolulu, gave me, I admit frankly, more pain than everything I have had to suffer since my childhood."[16]

Still Damien prayed on and struggled with his burden. In a notebook of spiritual reflections the missionary priest observed:

Let us be grateful to those who cause us pain or treat us with scorn, and pray to God for them. To accomplish this, beyond grace there is needed a great self-abnegation and a continual mortification; by these one finds oneself transformed into Christ crucified. St. John of the Cross always prayed: "Lord, may I be scorned for love of you." Let us make frequent meditations on the scorn which Christ suffered before Pilate . . . .[17]

The dryness and darkness most of us experience in our prayer lives will not be as dramatic as those which Damien encountered. But the pain brought on by them can cause us to waver and even to falter in our commitment to regular praying.

Yet merely to understand the naturalness of those passive purifications and even to expect them may encourage us to persevere in prayer. As one of my workshop participants wrote afterward: "You cleared up some self-doubt that I had about my prayer life. Sometimes it will be hard to pray, but I should continue to do so, because it still is prayer."

I might add—very likely pure and powerful prayer at that.

Reflective Prayer Suggestions

1. Read through the triple prediction of Jesus' paschal mystery in one of the Synoptic Gospels and note the miracle before and teaching afterward (Matthew 16:21–23; 17:22–23; 20:17–19; Mark 8:31–33; 9:30–32; 10:32–34; Luke 9:22; 9:43–45; 18:31–33).

2. Reflect on an occasion when you prayed, experienced dryness or darkness, and how you reacted. Would your response be different now?

3. Consider how the rage for self-fulfillment in our culture has practically influenced your life or the lives of people close to you.

◇ *Principle #7:*

Good prayer must be cross stamped.

> They devoted themselves to the apostles' instruction and the communal life, to the breaking of bread and the prayers. A reverent fear overtook them all, for many wonders and signs were performed by the apostles. Those who believed shared all things in common; they would sell their property and goods, dividing everything on the basis of each one's need. They went to the temple area together every day, while in their homes they broke bread. With exultant and sincere hearts they took their meals in common, praising God and winning the approval of all the people. Day by day the Lord added to their number those who were being saved (Acts 2:42–47).

The term "cross stamped" may seem to indicate that good prayer must always begin with the sign of the cross or concentrate on the crucifix of Calvary or center itself around Christ. Each of those elements certainly is praiseworthy and can help a person pray more effectively.

Nevertheless, I use the phrase "cross stamped" here instead as an easy way of remembering that good prayer should include two dimensions—a vertical thrust directed to God and at the same time a horizontal movement toward fellow humans.

◇ Thus, people who pray well should possess a spirit or attitude of standing in awe and need before our great God above who is the transcendent One, the totally Other, the all-powerful, wise, just, merciful, loving and provident Creator.

At the same time those who pray well also must possess a spirit or attitude of genuine concern about and awareness of other humans as brothers and sisters.

◇ We ought, as it were, simultaneously to fold our hands in reverence before the Lord and to stretch out those same hands to persons around us.

◊ In good prayer we travel upward on the vertical bar of the cross toward the Lord, expressing our praise and adoration while also waiting with open hearts for God's response to our requests.

Such good prayer, however, likewise moves along the cross' horizontal bar toward neighbors near and far who claim our affection, attention and assistance.

◊ That excerpt above from the Acts of the Apostles which describes the life of the early Christians reflects this cross stamped approach to prayer and worship.

They possessed a reverential fear in the face of God's many wonders and signs worked among them by the apostles; they broke bread (celebrated the Eucharist) and prayed; they went daily to the temple for worship; they praised God with exultant and sincere hearts. Clearly these first followers of Jesus had a vertical element in their inner attitudes and public prayer.

But those initial Christians also embraced a community life style; they shared all things in common; they sold property and goods, dividing them among the needy; they approached the temple for joint worship not as individuals, but together; they also celebrated the Eucharist and took their meals at homes in common; they welcomed converts to Christ and the Church as new members of a caring, believing and praying spiritual family linked together by identical grace and faith. Obviously these beginning disciples of the Lord likewise maintained a horizontal dimension in their inner attitudes and external worship.

The cross, of course, intersects, and it is at that center point where we achieve an integration of both bars or a proper balance of the transcendent and the communal. Good prayer thus will seek to blend appropriately each of these thrusts, one upward and the other outward.

Achieving such a balanced combination is an on-going challenge, one that Christians have struggled with throughout the Church's history. There seems to be within humans a constant, strong tendency to move excessively in one direction or the other and in that process to lose a proper perspective. Moreover, this inclination to err in one way or the other, to emphasize one aspect at the expense of another, holds true not only for the practical way we do things in the Church like worship, but also for the intellectual manner with which we conceive of God.

The practical and intellectual are, of course, closely related. The way in which we look at or understand God will impact the style of our prayer. Our prayer, on the other hand, reflects and helps mold our concept of the Lord.

What complicates all this is the fact that God, the Trinity, Jesus, the Church, the sacraments and even ourselves are mysteries which we never fully fathomed. We cannot plumb the depths or totally grasp with our finite minds any of these realities. That leaves humans restless and discontented. We do not enjoy ambiguity, gray areas or partially understood truths. Such restlessness and discontent, therefore, may compel us to take one side or the other, to exaggerate one aspect or the other and, consequently, to remove the troublesome grayness or ambiguity. But in so doing we muddy the waters, acquire a false understanding of some theological truth and slip into unhealthy spiritual practices.

An overview of theological trends and pastoral procedures during the past thirty years or so should clarify these generalized statements.

Prior to the Second Vatican Council, there was an inclination among some to view God almost entirely from a transcendent, awesome, fear-inspiring viewpoint. Prayer, public and private, mirrored this approach to the Lord. There was heavy emphasis on mystery in worship, nearly no vocal participation and an individualized, highly personal style of prayer.

For example, when I was ordained in 1956 I offered Mass with my back to the people. The congregation read from their missals, recited their beads or contemplated in reverence the holy action before them. There was no response from the congregation except one morning when my server dropped the glass cruets on our marble cathedral altar. He uttered a single word comment not untypical for such accidents which the public address system carried throughout that church. Those present did react then. Moreover, individuals in church during liturgy came forward from time to time, lit candles at the front, knelt down for private prayer, and remained quite oblivious of the Mass going on.

The liturgical and religious education reforms inspired by the Second Vatican Council drastically altered both that approach to God and the way we prayed.

Jesus Christ began to be seen more clearly as our brother, God as the caring Father and the Holy Spirit as dwelling within us. I now faced the congregation who at least recited the appropriate response and perhaps even sang the suitable hymns. We emphasized community celebrations of everything. Candle lighting individuals in the midst of liturgies became rather rare, and their infrequent appearances often provoked humor or irritation among on-looking clergy and congregation.

We could say, in an oversimplified view, that the vertical or "I" dimension of theology and prayer dominated the scene prior to the Second Vatican Council and that the horizontal or "We" aspect has held sway during the two decades since then.

In recent years several observers have begun to question whether the pendulum in theological emphasis and public prayer has not moved too far in one direction and should return a bit toward the center.

James DiGiacomo, a Jesuit priest, expended a good bit of time and energy as an educator in the 1960's and 1970's helping Catholics young and old move away from that excessive "I" and fear or distant approach to prayer and God. He wrote, taught and spoke about the "We" dimensions of worship and the loving, caring Lord who we believe is our friend.

It is, therefore, very significant to read DiGiacomo's comments and reservations about our current situation:

> But if the changing picture of God among adults is varied and ambiguous, it is remarkably homogeneous in its manifestations among the young. I believe that, at this moment in the American Catholic experience, we can state categorically that the great majority of young people see God not as Creator, Lord and Judge, but as Friend, Lover and Companion. Their religious experience is much more horizontal than vertical. Certain expressions occur over and over again. They say they don't like a religion that "puts God on a pedestal"; they don't like to think of Him as almighty sovereign. Their reaction to a film in which Bob Newhart portrays God is nearly always the same:

they like Newhart's God because he's so ordinary, so self-effacing, so much "on our level."[1]

Basically pleased with this shift from the Creator, Lord and Judge vision of God to the Friend, Lover and Companion notion, DiGiacomo then moves on to an uneasy reservation he has been experiencing:

Now this is very interesting. These young people seem to have gotten the message, much better than their parents did, that Jesus worked so hard to get across: that His Father is a loving, gentle friend who wants to be called Abba-"Daddy." On the other hand, I am uncomfortable with the idea of bringing God completely down to my level. I want him "on a pedestal," in some sense, at least. He is the Almighty, the Lord of the Universe, the All-Holy One, the God who is totally other, before whom the angels bow down in reverential awe.[2]

The Jesuit educator concludes with a call for catechesis in this decade which will bring back to center, integrate and balance the true notion of God.

Catechesis in the 1980's must build on what is best in the religion of young people and challenge them to aim higher. Assure them that their warm, friendly Lover God is indeed the true God, but that He is also the all-holy, sovereign Creator who is infinitely above us even as He reaches down to share our lot. Don't argue with them when they say that "all you need is love." But show them what real love is, more than a rub and a tickle, more than a vague warm feeling of benevolence without focus or direction. Tell them that love makes demands; that it costs; that sometimes it hurts. That it leads to a Cross.[3]

Father DiGiacomo teaches at Fordham University on the east coast. Across the continent on the west coast, Dr. Frederick J. Parrella instructs in religious studies at the University of Santa Clara. Writing about the same time in *The Christian Century*, Parrella makes an identical point about contemporary Catholic eucharistic celebrations that his Jesuit colleague stressed about Catholic religious education.

> Before Vatican II, liturgy was out of touch with modern experience; now, however, the pendulum has perhaps swung too far in the opposite direction, reducing the liturgy to a product of such experience.[4]

Parrella sees the need to bring back into Catholic worship a proper sense of transcendence. He would like to restore the vertical dimension, which creates in us an understanding of our unworthiness and sinfulness coupled with a clear appreciation of God's love. In his judgment disciples of Christ described in the Scriptures possessed that attitude. "Those in the New Testament who were deeply attracted to Jesus also felt great awe before him, a sense of distance between their sinfulness and his utter goodness."[5]

He summarizes his recommendations for a resurgence of this vertical element in prayer and worship with these words:

> I am not proposing a new otherwordly piety in our liturgy but simply a re-creation of holiness and transcendence in liturgical form. Without a sense of the Holy, we cannot pray, ask forgiveness, worship, be filled with gratitude before God's grace or, most significantly, know each other as brother and sister, which is God's gift in everyone to everyone else.[6]

Whether DiGiacomo and Parrella are right or wrong, whether pre-Vatican II approaches were too much one way and post-Vatican II attitudes now are excessive the other, is not really that significant. Our concern centers more on the fact that what we believe about God and how we pray to the Lord should follow a middle road, a balanced view, a cross stamped approach.

Saints of past ages and holy persons today have consistently blended these vertical and horizontal dimensions in their prayer and the Christian life.

St. Paul in the first Christian century, as we have seen, both urged his listeners to, and practiced himself, "constant prayer." "I give thanks to my God every time I think of you—which is constantly, in every prayer I utter—rejoicing, as I plead on your behalf . . . " (Philippians 1:3–4). As we shall note in the next part, he also joined with others in public prayers of praise. "About midnight, while Paul and Silas were praying and singing hymns to God as their fellow prisoners listened . . . " (Acts 16:25).

Paul not only prayed with others, he also found space in prayer to mention there the needs of his brothers and sisters. We find frequent instances of such interventions and even see how this concern spilled over into actual deeds of service. Those helping measures included, to illustrate, very pragmatic, down to earth efforts like the collection for the poor Christians of Jerusalem (Acts 24:17; Romans 15:25ff; 1 Corinthians 16; 2 Corinthians 8; Galatians 2:10).

The apostle to the Gentiles, therefore, prayed individually to the great God above, also united with fellow Christians in praise of the Father, and, finally, always kept the concerns of others in his prayer. He wedded well the vertical and horizontal.

Over a thousand years later, **St. Francis of Assisi** (1181?–1226), called by some the most perfect disciple of Jesus, pursued the same cross stamped prayer approach of St. Paul.

He eloquently praised God for the sun and the moon, for birds and flowers, but at the same time he gave everything he possessed to a poor beggar. He actively preached the Gospel throughout the Mediterranean world, but regularly withdrew alone to a wild, secluded, mountainous spot for long periods of private prayer. He spoke with Popes, cardinals and bishops about the reform of the Church, but off by himself became transfigured in ecstasy, even receiving the wounds of Christ stamped upon his hands, feet and side. He wrote a Rule for his followers and joined regularly with them for prayer, inspiration, work and companionship, but at times stepped aside for moments of individual contemplation.[7]

In the last century two women followed similar cross stamped prayer lives, but under quite different circumstances and with totally diverse ministries for others.

St. Elizabeth Ann Seton (1774–1821) was raised in New York City by a staunch Episcopalian who taught her the value of prayer, Scripture and a nightly examination of conscience. She married at nineteen a handsome, wealthy businessman and bore him five children, only to watch both his business and his health fail, leaving her a thirty year old, penniless widow.

Mother Seton's experience of Catholicism in Italy at the time of her husband's death, including belief in the Real Eucharistic Presence and devotion to the Blessed Mother, led her then to become a Catholic. She subsequently worked furiously at developing parochial schools in the United States and religious communities of sisters to carry on that educational task.

Her forty-seven years on earth included many deep trials— sickness, misunderstanding, premature death of loved ones and anxiety over a wayward son. Yet throughout both these burdens and those energetic labors for others, Mother Seton survived spiritually because of two basic devotions: a total abandonment to God's will and an ardent love for the Blessed Sacrament.[8]

St. Thérèse of the Child Jesus (1873–1897) lived less than half as long as did Mother Seton, and unlike St. Elizabeth Ann hardly traveled beyond the confines of the cloistered Carmelite convent in Lisieux, France.

She entered this religious community at the age of fifteen, knowing that her life would be routine and uneventful, consisting mainly of prayer and hard domestic work. Nevertheless, the Little Flower, as St. Thérèse came to be known, clearly saw the value of prayer and suffering for others. The young nun once remarked that she entered a Carmelite convent "to save souls and pray for priests." St. Thérèse also believed that "to pick up a pin for love can convert a soul."

The Little Flower's brief life seemed given over entirely to vertical prayer, to hours of individual adoration of God. Yet she did join often in that praise with her convent companions. Moreover, her heart and mind constantly moved beyond the cloistered walls to hurting persons out there in need of prayer. Because of this reaching out, horizontal, communal dimension in St. Thérèse's prayer life, the Holy Father eventually designated her as Patroness of the Missions.[9]

Finally, during this century and in our own day we have a man and a woman who illustrate the cross stamped approach.

St. Maximilian Kolbe (1894–1941) surely never anticipated when he became a Franciscan priest in Poland how he would ultimately die, nor would he have expected to be canonized a mere forty years after his death.

The story of this man's heroic offer of himself in a German concentration camp as a hostage destined to die in place of a family man is well known since Pope John Paul II declared him a saint on October 10, 1982.

The heroism displayed in Auschwitz, however, was merely the natural culmination of an ascetical, active and prayerful life. Father Kolbe always maintained an intense devotion to Mary, the Mother of God, and exhibited prior to incarceration a remarkable zeal in trying to promote love for the Blessed Virgin around the world.

After volunteering himself as a substitute, the Polish priest and nine other hostages were taken to an underground bunker condemned to die by starvation.

Bruno Borgowiec, an Auschwitz inmate who also served as official undertaker, secretary and interpreter, recalled after World War II the situation in that death cell and the last days of Maximilian Kolbe. To the end he prayed to God, helped others lift up their hearts to the Lord and brought strength to his dying companions:

> From the cell where these unfortunates were buried alive, you could hear the sound of prayers recited out loud, and the condemned men from other cells would join in. I had to go down once a day to accompany the guards on their inspection tour.
>
> Every time I went down there, I was greeted by fervent prayers and hymns to the holy Virgin whose sound pervaded the whole underground chamber. Father Maximilian would start them out; then everyone joined in.
>
> Sometimes they would be so absorbed in prayer that they did not even realize the guards had come for the daily inspection and had opened their cell door. Only when the SS began shouting at them would they stop praying.
>
> To give you an idea of what these prisoners went through, I need only mention that I never needed to empty the bucket

in the corner (for urine). It was always empty and dry. The prisoners actually drank its contents in order to satisfy their thirst.

Father Kolbe displayed real heroism. He asked for nothing and did not complain.

After the first week, they were so weak they had to recite their prayers in a whisper. Though the others were helplessly prone on the floor, Father Kolbe still greeted the SS inspectors while standing or kneeling among the others, a look of serenity on his face.

The guards knew he had volunteered his life in place of the prisoner who had a family. Once I heard one of them say: "This priest is a real man. I never saw one like him here before."[10]

Mother Teresa of Calcutta needs no introduction. In 1952 she came across an abandoned woman dying in the streets of that Indian city and being eaten up by rats and ants. She picked up the lady and sought help for her both at a local hospital and from city authorities. When neither could respond to her plea, the nun accepted a building they offered and began the next day to provide a home for the destitute sick and dying.

Today there are three thousand Mother Teresas in fifty-two countries doing what she did. These women, members of her Missionaries of Charity, have joined this religious community to give "wholehearted, free service to the poorest of the poor." They are seeking, in Mother Teresa's words, "a life of prayer, poverty and sacrifice."[11]

The frail, elderly woman in blue and white cotton sari models that style of living for her followers. When press corps representatives one day pressed Mother Teresa to explain the motivation behind her inspirational work for the poorest of the poor, she cited three sources: love for Jesus; devotion to the Eucharist; daily, prolonged prayer.[12]

Mother Teresa's integration of the vertical and horizontal elements in prayer and living, like that of all her predecessors noted above, should come as no surprise. She and each of them is or was a disciple of Jesus who similarly combined praying to the Father, praying with others and praying for others. We described Christ as such a prayer model for us in Principle #1; readers will find a further delineation of the Lord as an example of prayer in the Appendix, paragraphs 3–4.

How can we in a practical way make certain that our prayer is cross stamped, blending the transcendent and the communal or adoration of our God above with concern for people around us? Here are a few suggestions.

Treat symbols in prayer and worship with care and awe.

Missionary Benedictine monks established Blue Cloud Abbey outside of Marvin, South Dakota many years ago to serve the spiritual needs of Native Americans living on a nearby Indian reservation. A stained glass window in the handsome abbey chapel contains an ancient saying of St. Benedict, the community's founder: "Work, read and pray."

During the week from about 8:30 to 11:10 and from 1:30 to 5:00, the men at Blue Cloud carry out that first injunction. They look after beef cattle, tend huge fields of wheat or corn, repair farm equipment, maintain the buildings, perform clerical tasks or care for countless bee hives which produce the five to ten tons of honey sold each year.

But within the remaining hours of each day, these Benedictines fulfill their founder's other directives: read and pray. They may find a quiet, secluded spot in the woods for reflective spiritual reading or assemble in chapel for common singing of the Liturgy of the Hours.

Both activities radiate a quality of carefulness and awe. The way a monk sits by the stream or underneath some tree with book in hand reflects an awareness of God's presence. An observer senses that the meditating Benedictine is in silent, prayerful communion with the Lord of all creation. The way they pray communally the Liturgy of the Hours likewise manifests real care and a sense of awe. The slow pace of their singing, the solemnity of their bows and the respectfulness of their silent pauses convey a similar attitude of comfortable but awesome wonder before the Almighty.

St. Benedict also cautioned: "Prefer nothing to the praise of God." It is evident these monks take that admonition seriously, working energetically each day, but never letting that physical or mental labor interfere with their public or private prayer.

Most religious symbols—objects, words or gestures—can through frequent repetition become routine and, consequently, lose much of their power. For example, the sign of the cross, bows, genuflections, the Bible, sacramental items like bread, wine and water, prayer words or formulas—any of these if made or used without attention or awareness may deteriorate into mere external gestures not capable of touching our minds or hearts. We need to bring, as the Blue Cloud monks do, those inner attitudes of care and awe to such symbols.

Provide ample moments of silence in private or public prayer.

Each week during the summer months, over one thousand young people between the ages of eighteen and twenty-five, camp for a week outside the ecumenical community of Taizé in southern France. Every day, for about an hour in the morning and a half hour in the late afternoon, these youth join with the Taizé members for a period of prayer. Both sessions follow an overall structure or pattern, but also provide great freedom and flexibility. They thus offer opportunities for reading, singing, petitions and silent reflection. Those times of silence, however, are essential for the spirit of prayerfulness which emerges and dominates that religious group in France. It is that spirit and the emphasis on silent prayer which, among other factors, attracts such a remarkable number of youthful Europeans to Taizé.

So, too, our liturgical worship or personal prayer requires substantial pauses for silent reflection. We need the opportunity to listen as well as to speak, to hear what God is saying to us within our hearts as well as to express silently to the Lord what is going on inside of us.

Pray alone, but also with others both mentally and physically.

Principle #1 of this part strongly urged a daily period of prolonged prayer, a time set aside specifically for an individual to be alone with God. However, if we only pray in isolation and by ourselves, there is danger that our prayer will become unhealthily self-centered. As social beings we likewise need to join with fellow believers for worship.

Pre-Vatican II people did that. We regularly went to Mass and often attended other services. Nevertheless, while there existed a physical togetherness, in many ways those congregations more truly represented merely a group of isolated individuals gathered together in one location for a common ceremony. As we noted above, people at the Eucharist recited the rosary, followed their English missals or simply gazed at the action in the sanctuary. Sunday Mass offered us an hour out of the week where in the quiet of church and away from work or family pressures, we could half pray along with the liturgy and half reflect with God on the current status of our lives.

I believe therein lies the explanation for some of the resistance to the introduction of certain Vatican II community-building steps in the liturgy like the sign of peace and congregational singing. Official documents can teach that "liturgical services are not private functions, but are celebrations of the Church . . . ." They might urge that "rites which are meant to be celebrated in common, with the faithful present and actively participating, should as far as possible be celebrated in that way rather than by an individual and quasi-privately."[13] But decades of a private, individualized tradition create habits not easily broken or transformed.

The point is that a person seeking to grow in prayer must come to recognize the importance of not only being physically present with others for worship, but also, at the same time, of being spiritually or mentally present with and to others during such prayer. Their minds and hearts, not the body alone, should be one with and to the entire congregation.

When that occurs, our personal, private and individualized prayer feeds and stimulates our communal prayer; conversely, our active conscious participation in common, public prayer nourishes and deepens those occasions either within silent moments of group worship or when off by ourselves we pray individually and privately.

A few examples of prayer together come to mind: Sunday worship, of course; reciting or singing the Liturgy of the Hours; common praying of the rosary; the regular meeting of prayer groups; celebrating various sacramental moments like baptisms, weddings and funerals; even uniting with others for meditation or centering prayer.

Joining fully with sisters and brothers in worship thus neutralizes a tendency toward excessive self-centeredness and fosters a spirit of charity, of love reaching out toward others.

Pray for others.

I can still remember clearly a large picture which hung in my bedroom during childhood days. In soft but somber colors it captured a pensive, sad Jesus looking over the city of Jerusalem. Years later, when touring the Holy Land, that painting came back to my mind as I walked down Mount Olivet and stopped at what is termed the "Dominus Flevit" chapel.

This small but attractive structure halfway down the hill from Bethphage and Bethany toward Jerusalem overlooks the ancient city. Mass can be celebrated on an altar in it facing the walls of that famous metropolis. During sunny periods the view from there is spectacular.

The Latin "Dominus Flevit" means "The Lord wept," and the chapel has been so designated because it commemorates the following incident of Jesus' life:

> Coming in sight of the city, he wept over it and said: "If only you had known the path to peace this day; but you have lost it completely from view! Days will come upon you when your enemies encircle you with a rampart, hem you in, and press you hard from every side. They will wipe you out, you and your children within your walls, and leave not a stone on a stone within you, because you failed to recognize the time of your visitation" (Luke 19:41–44).

This episode presents for me a graphic illustration of Christ's prayerful concern for others. I imagine Jesus here not only expressing his sorrowful anguish and regretful warning about Jerusalem's impending destruction, but at the same time praying to his Father about those hostile people and their perilous situation.

Our prayer needs to follow that pattern. While we may and should speak to God about our own personal needs, we likewise need regularly to bring the concerns of others into our prayer. Like communal prayer, that type of reaching out prayer will help us avoid the dangerous, self-centered approach which can be so destructive.

When we find space within us for another's needs and pray for that individual, it expands our heart and softens it. By consciously taking the person who troubles, worries, alienates or hurts us into our prayer we normally will find a diminishing or dissolving of the anxiety, alienation or resentment connected with that person.

Prayer for others produces peace within us as Jesus promised: "Peace is my farewell to you, my peace is my gift to you" (John 14:27).

The second paragraph of the Constitution on the Sacred Liturgy speaks about the mystery of Christ and the Church. In describing the nature of the true Church, it states that the Church is "essentially both human and divine, visible but endowed with invisible realities, zealous in action and dedicated to contemplation, present in the world, but as a pilgrim, so constituted that in her the human is directed toward and subordinated to the divine, the visible to the invisible, action to contemplation, and this present world to that city yet to come, the object of our quest."[14]

Good prayer, like the Church, blends the human and divine, action and contemplation, the vertical and the horizontal, the transcendent and the communal, the here and now with the yet to come.

In the next part we will examine seven common types of prayer, seven shapes that good prayer may take, seven styles all of which can or should be cross stamped.

Reflective Prayer Suggestions

1. Reflect on the excerpt from the Acts of the Apostles at the beginning of this section (2:42–47) and its companion paragraph (4:32–35). How does the prayerful attitude of these early Christians compare with your own and that of your family, parish or worshiping community?

2. Read paragraphs 3–5 in the appendix from the General Instruction of the Liturgy of the Hours and ponder how Jesus prayed alone, with and for others. If you have time, look up in the New Testament some of the footnotes there and continue your meditation.

3. Examine your own prayer life in the light of this principle #7. Do you see a need for change? If so, how can you improve? What practical step or steps do you intend to make to enhance your prayer?

== *Part II:*
Seven Different Ways of Praying

The seven quite diverse methods of prayer described in this part do not exhaust the ways people pray. Neither are they necessarily the best styles of prayer nor does the order in which we treat them here indicate some hierarchy of excellence among those methods. Each way of praying has proven very satisfactory for many people and a good number of persons use several or all of them in their regular prayer lives. For those already familiar with a particular method we hope the explanation below will make it a richer way of praying; for those unfamiliar with a particular style we hope the description which follows will open up to them a new avenue or possibility for speaking and listening to the Lord. We have listed a few helpful published resources at the end of each section describing a specific way of praying.

◇ *Method #1:*

Mary and the Rosary

In this chapter, I will first discuss the current resurgence of interest in Mary and Marian devotions, then present an outline history of the rosary, and, finally, suggest some practical tips for effectively praying the "beads."

The Resurgence of Mary

When very dissimilar Catholic periodicals within a few months' time carry totally unrelated but similar articles agreeing on a certain point, it would seem both that there must be some truth in the assertion and that the silent, mysterious action of the Holy Spirit is present.

In the relatively recent past three publications we might label, Churchwise, as center, left and right (although such designations for anything or any person are simplistic and should be avoided) have printed articles on Mary. The essays spoke about the importance, rediscovery and liberation of the Blessed Virgin.

The editors of *Catholic Twin Circle*, a national weekly magazine, would probably be comfortable with its designation as a journal with a "right" orientation. The periodical stresses regard for the traditions of Catholicism and questions the validity of some Church changes.

The January 10, 1982 issue contained an article, "Why Young Catholics Leave the Church—and Return." That story summarized major findings of a current sociological study about youthful Catholics in the United States and Canada. In response to a question on what, apart from marriage, prompts such Catholics to return to the Church, the author gave this interesting reply:

"A warm image of Our Lady was found to be of prime importance. The study found that 81 per cent of young Catholics thought of Mary the Madonna as 'gentle' and had a warm image of her . . . ."[1]

The editors of *Commonweal*, a bi-weekly review of public affairs, literature and the arts, would probably accept the labeling of their journal as "left" on Church matters. It terms itself a periodical of liberal thought and would urge the implementation or expansion of changes decreed by the Second Vatican Council.

The January 15, 1982 issue includes an article by the well-known contemporary novelist Mary Gordon (*Final Payments* and *The Company of Women*) on "Coming to Terms with Mary."

Gordon sketches some of her high school encounters with teachings on the Virgin Mary and how she found it necessary then to reject certain images of Our Lady which were projected at that period.

After experiencing motherhood for the first time, however, the novelist yearned to regain a relationship with Jesus' mother and create for herself a devotion to Mary that "honors her as woman, as mother, that rejects the wickedness of sexual hatred and sexual fear."

She discovered this kind of image about and devotion toward Our Lady centering around three words: innocence, grief and glory. Her article develops those notions and concludes with these strong statements: "Devotion to Mary is the objective correlative of all the primitive desires that lead human beings to the life of faith. She embodies our desire to be fully human yet to transcend death . . . . In Mary, Mother and Queen, we see, enfleshed in a human form that touches our most ancient longings, the promise of salvation, of deliverance, through flesh, from the burdens of flesh."[2]

The editors of *Notre Dame Magazine*, the alumni journal which has over the past few years become a truly outstanding publication, would probably be content with the categorization that it steers a "center" course.

The December 1981 issue carried an article on "The Liberation of Mary" by Sally Cunneen, a founding editor of the theological journal *Cross Currents*.

She begins, "I often wonder how many Catholics, after the Second Vatican Council, quietly put away their rosaries—but now feel like dragging them out again . . . . Many of us tucked away our rosaries and our images of Mary, hoping someday to reconcile our childhood devotions with the challenges of a changing world and a changing Church.

"I think the time for that reconciliation has come. Many Catholics recently have begun to see that Jesus' mother has more to do with our reality than we once thought. Now we need a new understanding of Mary which allows us to reclaim her."[3]

That consensus about the resurgence of interest in Mary and Marian devotions received printed confirmation a little over one year later in *America*, the Jesuit national Catholic weekly magazine.

Mitch Finley, a free-lance writer from Spokane, Washington, described his own experience of "Recovering the Rosary."

> I have taken to praying the rosary again. It must be a good dozen years since I last prayed in this particular "mode" (as they say), and there is a sense of homecoming (I did not say nostalgia) about it. There's one thing about the rosary: It has "Catholic" written all over it.[4]

Finley apparently touched some responsive chords in readers because a month afterward several letters to the editor appeared with positive comments indicating that the rosary has both an international and ecumenical dimension to it.

From Pennsylvania one woman spoke of the rosary's value for a Philippine patient critically ill with cancer:

> As a hospice nurse, I spend a great deal of time with people who are dying or are close to death. One was a young Philippine woman dying of cancer. She was a fairly recent arrival in Philadelphia, and the nurses taking care of her were not sure if she knew how ill she was or that she would not get home to see her year-old baby again.
>
> I went in to see her one night. She was too weak to talk, and I sat with her. She had a rosary at her bedside, and I asked her if she wanted me to say the rosary with her. She nodded "yes" but was too weak to answer so I said all the prayers.
>
> The first time I said "pray for us, now and at the hour of

our death," she opened her eyes and looked at me with such
knowledge and understanding that I knew too well she knew
she was dying.[5]

From Arlington, Texas a clergyman from St. Bartholomew's
Episcopal Church noted that the rosary may indeed be a "Catholic" devotion, but in fact many outside the Roman Catholic Church
treasure and use it:

> I was happy to read Mitch Finley's "Recovering the Rosary."
> As he says, it has "Catholic" written all over it. But I would
> just like to add that the rosary is widely used and valued by
> Catholics who are in exile from the Roman obedience.
>
> The rosary has long been recited daily in the Holy House
> at the (Anglican) Shrine of Our Lady of Walsingham in Eng-
> land. It is said that John Wesley always had a rosary with him
> as he traveled on his preaching missions. And perhaps the best
> book in recent years on the mysteries of the rosary is *Five for
> Sorrow, Ten for Joy* by Neville Ward, who is himself a Meth-
> odist minister—though I doubt that this implies a widespread
> use of the rosary among Methodists.
>
> It is a different matter, however, among Episcopalians.
> And T.S. Eliot, from whom Mitch Finley quotes, was himself
> an Episcopalian.[6]

It would be a generally agreed upon observation and one illustrated by several of these articles or letters that the place of
Mary and Marian devotions among Roman Catholics suffered a
decline in practice after the Second Vatican Council. Why that de-
terioration actually occurred is a complex question and I do not
pretend to answer it in this book. Nevertheless conciliar documents and later official teachings strongly continued to uphold the
position of Mary in the Church and encouraged devotions, even
though revised ones, to honor the Mother of Jesus.

Father Eamon Carroll, a scholar whose specialty is the study
of Mary, comments that "the conciliar teaching on the Virgin
Mary began with the first decree, on the liturgy (December 1963),
peaked in the chapter on Mary in the Dogmatic Constitution on
the Church (November 1964) and found expression in still other

statements on Our Lady—in twelve of the total sixteen documents."[7]

A crucial paragraph, no. 67, from that Dogmatic Constitution on the Church provides an excellent summary on Marian devotions. It reinforces their rightful spot in the Church, yet cautions that they should always have a connection or a reference to Christ.

> The Sacred Synod teaches this Catholic doctrine advisedly and at the same time admonishes all the sons of the Church that the cult, especially the liturgical cult, of the Blessed Virgin, be generously fostered, and that the practices and exercises of devotion toward her, recommended by the teaching authority of the Church in the course of centuries, be highly esteemed, and that those decrees, which were given in the early days regarding the cult images of Christ, the Blessed Virgin and the saints, be religiously observed. But it strongly urges theologians and preachers of the word of God to be careful to refrain as much from all false exaggeration as from too summary an attitude in considering the special dignity of the Mother of God. Following the study of Sacred Scripture, the Fathers, the Doctors and the liturgy of the Church, and under the guidance of the Church's magisterium, let them rightly illustrate the duties and privileges of the Blessed Virgin which always refer to Christ, the source of all truth, sanctity, and devotion. Let them carefully refrain from whatever might by word or deed lead the separated brethren or any others whatsoever into error about the true doctrine of the Church. Let the faithful remember moreover that true devotion consists neither in sterile or transistory affection, nor in a certain vain credulity, but proceeds from true faith, by which we are led to recognize the excellence of the Mother of God, and we are moved to a filial love toward our mother and to the imitation of her virtues.[8]

Two subsequent official teachings of the Church expand upon this conciliar doctrine about Mary.

On November 21, 1973 the National Conference of Catholic Bishops in the United States published, *Behold Your Mother: Woman of Faith*, "A Pastoral Letter on the Blessed Virgin Mary."[9] It summarized the current theological understanding of

Mary and provided pragmatic guidelines and suggestions for Marian devotions.

Months afterward, on February 2, 1974, Pope Paul VI issued *Marialis Cultus*, an apostolic exhortation for the right ordering and development of devotion to the Blessed Virgin Mary.[10] It, too, examined the theology of Mary and offered practical recommendations for two devotions in particular—the Angelus and the rosary.

The Church, therefore, has constantly maintained the value of Marian devotions, including and in a special way the rosary. In actual practice, after the Second Vatican Council Catholics seemed to put aside and minimize those types of prayer. Now, however, that trend appears to have reversed with more and more Roman Catholics as well as others rediscovering the importance of Mary in their lives and the riches of Marian devotion, especially the rosary.

A History of the Rosary

To trace the origin and development of an ancient religious practice like the rosary is not an easy nor entirely successful task. Both the beginnings and the gradual shaping date back 1000–1500 years when historical records and accounts of popular devotions were less accurate or detailed than today. My summary which follows thus is not *the* history, but merely *a* history of the rosary based on a small, hard-cover devotional book.[11]

Most historians trace the rosary's origin back to the fifth through the ninth century in Ireland. Those in monastic life at the time daily recited or chanted the 150 Psalms. Lay people outside the monasteries were impressed by this practice, but without books and the ability to read they could not join the monks or nuns in such prayer.

At one point in this period a monk suggested to the neighboring lay people that they recite a series of 150 Our Fathers just as the monastic community prays the 150 Psalms. Many liked the recommendation, adopted it, but subsequently needed to fashion some system for counting the 150 Our Fathers.

Initially they carried leather pouches which could hold 150 pebbles. Then these lay folk made ropes with 150 or 50 knots on them. Eventually they commonly employed strings which linked together 50 pieces of wood.

St. Peter Damian, who died in 1072, mentioned that both the clergy and laity had begun to recite as a repetitive prayer the Angelic Salutation which forms most of the first part of the Hail Mary. Consequently, there now existed side by side two similar, but different devotions—repeating 50 or 150 either Our Fathers or Angelic Salutations.

During the medieval period, theologians began to see in the Psalms veiled prophecies of Jesus' life, death and resurrection. By the thirteenth century they had created a series of 150 praises in honor of Christ based upon these interpretations of the Psalms. It was only a matter of time until a parallel collection of 150 praises of Mary had been composed.

It was around this century that such a practice of counting the beads came to be termed a "round" or "chaplet" or "little crown" of prayers honoring Mary. When only 50 instead of 150 Marian praises or Angelic Salutations were prayed, people commonly called this a "rosarium," a rose garden or bouquet for the Blessed Virgin.[12]

In 1365 Henry of Kalkar, the Carthusian Order Visitator, first combined the Paters and Aves by grouping the 150 Angelic Salutations into decades with an Our Father before each decade.

About a half century later, around 1409, another Carthusian, Dominic the Prussian, wrote a book with 50 thoughts about the lives of Jesus and Mary for attachment to a rosary. Subsequently, his contribution was modified and expanded until by 1470 a Dominican, Alan of Rupe, promoted a "new" rosary with a special thought for each Hail Mary bead.

This Dominican established the first Rosary Confraternity, a step which also launched the Dominican Order as the foremost missionaries of the rosary.

By the sixteenth and seventeenth centuries, that practice of reciting the rosary with a thought for each bead gradually died out, but the major reason for this decline is rather interesting. Around 1500 it became possible to reproduce wood cut picture prints inexpensively. Since the majority of lay folk still could not read, they warmly accepted new rosaries with pictures representing the thoughts for every bead. That proved awkward and costly for 150 different pictures. As a consequence, the picture rosaries came to include only one wood cut for each Our Father bead, although often all ten Hail Mary thoughts were printed around the Our Father image.

Fairly soon after the disappearance of the thought per bead practice, people recognized a need to augment the fifteen brief mystery statements. That recognition spawned the composition of meditations read before each decade, the most popular of which St. Louis de Montfort wrote around 1700. We can recognize variations on this approach in the common Catholic procedure over the past half century of a few meditative words given by the leader following the announcement of each mystery.

Currently there are some efforts to resurrect the older tradition of a thought for each bead or a more expansive introduction to every decade. We will mention them in the next section.

Several Practical Suggestions

I presume here that the reader understands the basic mechanics of reciting the rosary. However, if not, the booklet "Pray the Rosary" listed under Helpful Resources below could be very useful for anyone wishing to begin praying in this manner.

For those familiar with the rosary, however, the challenge is more how best to pray the "beads" and keep the devotion from becoming routine. We offer now a few suggestions to aid in preserving this method fresh and alive for us.

First of all, there are a few general attitudes or approaches which should always be present regardless of the specific technique we employ while praying the rosary.

◊ Mitch Finley from Spokane, whose recent rediscovery of the rosary we have noted above, describes some of those attitudes or approaches as he recounts his own pattern of using the "beads."

> The rosary can be easily incorporated into a contemporary incarnational or sacramental spirituality. The rosary involves a

grasping of material things (the beads) that other, more popular methods of prayer do not. Just sitting and attempting to empty oneself surely has its place. But there is something right about a way of prayer that gives you something to grab on to. To involve the sense of touch so fully in one's prayer is body-affirming. The fingers, among the most sensitive of the body's parts, pause on each bead, passing them through the hands like the moments of a lifetime, which are prayer.

When recited with others, the sense of hearing becomes involved, like an ear covered by a sea shell. The rhythmic ebb and flow of the repetitious prayers invokes a kind and prayerful spirit which nourishes not just tranquility, but trust and courage and hope.

Daily, once our three children are off to sleep, when dark has fallen, I take my regular walk around our urban neighborhood. I walk about a mile in one direction, then return by the same route. With beads held in my coat pocket, I walk, rather briskly, and pray. Once I have finished the rosary, I continue grasping the beads but I move over to the Jesus Prayer. Besides family and friends, others pass through my thoughts: those who hunger; those who are tortured or in prison; the strangers in the houses I pass (nearly all gazing into glowing television screens); children who, right here, have been beaten or abused by their beaten and abused parents. The list is, of course, quite endless. [13]

◇ Pope Paul VI observed that each element of the rosary possesses its own particular character which should be reflected in the manner we recite the rosary. Thus:

The recitation will be grave and suppliant during the Lord's Prayer, lyrical and full of praise during the tranquil succession of Hail Marys, contemplative in the recollected meditation on the mysteries and full of adoration during the doxology. This applies to all the ways in which the Rosary is usually recited: privately, in intimate recollection with the Lord; in community, in the family or in groups of the faithful gathered together to ensure the special presence of the Lord (cf. Mt 18:20); or publicly, in assemblies to which the ecclesial community is invited. [14]

◇ While seeing no contradiction between the liturgy and the rosary and, instead, urging their integration in one's spiritual life, the Holy Father also issues a direct and blunt disapproval of a somewhat common practice:

> In fact meditation on the mysteries of the rosary, by familiar-izing the hearts and minds of the faithful with the mysteries of Christ, can be an excellent preparation for the celebration of those same mysteries in the liturgical action and can also be-come a continuing echo thereof. However, it is a mistake to re-cite the rosary during the celebration of the liturgy, though unfortunately this practice still persists here and there.[15]

◇ Pope Paul VI likewise comments on the Gospel inspiration behind the rosary. He mentions how the fifteen mysteries—joy-ful, sorrowful and glorious—represent the entire life and work of Jesus, thus mirroring the mystery of Christ as preached by St. Paul to the Philippians:

> It has also been more easily seen how the orderly and gradual unfolding of the rosary reflects the very way in which the Word of God, mercifully entering into human affairs, brought about the redemption. The rosary considers in harmonious succes-sion the principal salvific events accomplished in Christ, from his virginal conception and the mysteries of his childhood to the culminating moments of the passover—the blessed passion and the glorious resurrection—and to the effects of this on the in-fant Church on the day of Pentecost, and on the Virgin Mary when at the end of her earthly life she was assumed body and soul into her heavenly home. It has also been observed that the division of the mysteries of the rosary into three parts not only adheres strictly to the chronological order of the facts but above all reflects the plan of the original proclamation of the faith and sets forth once more the mystery of Christ in the very way in which it is seen by Saint Paul in the celebrated "hymn" of the Letter to the Philippians—kenosis, death and exaltation (2:6–11).[16]

Secondly, with the assumption that the above attitudes or ap-proaches are always present when we recite the beads, here are several very practical techniques or ways of praying the rosary.

◊ **Meditating on the mysteries**. This has been the more commonly followed method among Catholics in the past decades.
We declare to ourselves or a leader announces to the group the
specific mystery about to be contemplated with or without
some explanation or comment. We then recite the Our Father,
ten Hail Marys and Glory to the Father all the time maintaining a picture of that mystery before our mind. This procedure
can be more or less humanly satisfying and successful, full or
free of distractions depending on many factors.

The "Pray the Rosary" pamphlet has ten points of meditation
for each decade or mystery to facilitate the contemplation during
one's recitation.

◊ **Scriptural Rosary**. This relatively recent devotional development builds on the medieval practice described in the preceding section which inserted a thought or phrase of praise before
each Hail Mary. It differs, however, from that approach because nearly all of the reflections prior to an Ave are biblically
based. In praying the scriptural rosary, one ponders the mystery announced in a general way while reciting the Our Father,
then reads the scriptural thought and follows with a Hail Mary,
repeating this process for the rest of the decade.

The *Scriptural Rosary* manual listed at the end, an attractive
publication, contains directions on how to pray the "beads" in this
way and supplies the biblical quotes.

◊ **Jesus and the Mystery**. Pope Paul VI recalls a tradition popular among some peoples of adding a reference to the specific
mystery after the word "Jesus" in the Hail Mary. He writes:
"As is well known, at one time there was a custom, still pre-
served in certain places, of adding to the name of Jesus in each
Hail Mary a reference to the mystery being contemplated. And
this was done precisely in order to help contemplation and to
make the mind and the voice act in unison."[17]

Thus, to illustrate, while praying the third joyful mystery,
the nativity, the prayer might move like this: " . . . .Blessed is the
fruit of thy womb, Jesus, who was born in Bethlehem."

◊ **The Family Rosary.** Mitch Finley describes how he, his wife and some other couples gathered one evening to pray and for some reason turned to the rosary as a vehicle for their common prayer.

> A few weeks ago, my wife and I joined eight other married couples for prayer. We began a series of gatherings to pray for marriage in general, and for marriages in particular—our own and those of couples we know who seem in need of some prayer right about now. A small purpose, really, but one with vast implications.
>
> We lit the living room with fluttering candles and, yes, prayed the rosary—not without self-consciousness, to be sure, since none of us had thought of ourselves as rosary types for a good long time.
>
> What a remarkable thing, I thought to myself. We gathered, greeted one another, and here we are right away praying. We did not spend several meetings trying to agree on how to pray, first.[18]

Pope Paul VI would applaud that effort on the part of those people from Spokane, Washington. He earlier had explicitly endorsed the practice of the family rosary:

> We now desire, as a continuation of the thought of our predecessors, to recommend strongly the recitation of the family rosary. The Second Vatican Council has pointed out how the family, the primary and vital cell of society, "shows itself to be the domestic sanctuary of the Church through the mutual affection of its members and the common prayer they offer to God." The Christian family is thus seen to be a domestic Church if its members, each according to his proper place and tasks, all together promote justice, practice works of mercy, devote themselves to helping their brethren, take part in the apostolate of the wider local community and play their part in its liturgical worship. This will be all the more true if together they offer up prayers to God. If this element of common prayer were missing, the family would lack its very character as a domestic Church. Thus there must logically follow a concrete effort to reinstate communal prayer in family life if there is to be

a restoration of the theological concept of the family as the domestic Church.[19]

◇ **A Person for Every Bead.** On occasion, especially when fatigued or pre-occupied, I find it helpful to recite each Hail Mary for a different person. Mentally I move from one individual to another—family, friends, parishioners, co-workers, world and religious leaders, people in special need—and pray an Ave for that one before my mind.

◇ **A Continent for Every Decade.** This is a variation of the previous approach. As I pray a decade, I think of the Church and the people on a particular continent with their needs, burdens and joys. That raises my consciousness of the universal Church and also helps me concentrate when my mind seems to wander all over the place.

◇ **Changing Posture.** In certain circumstances, like the family rosary or praying alone in church or with a group of people, it may be helpful to vary our posture—to kneel for the first decade, stand for the second, kneel for the third, etc.

◇ **Creative Approaches.** The American bishops in encouraging the rosary as a valuable aspect of our Catholic devotional life also suggested fresh and creative alternatives for its recitation, even urging us to conceive of additional ways to invigorate this particular prayer.

> The recommended saying of the rosary does not consist merely in "telling the beads" by racing through a string of familiar prayers. Interwoven with the prayers are the "mysteries." Almost all of these relate saving events in the life of Jesus, episodes in which the Mother of Jesus shared. Nor is rhythmic prayer alien to modern man, as is shown by the attraction of Eastern religions for many young people today. Besides the precise rosary pattern long known to Catholics, we can freely experiment. New sets of mysteries are possible. We have customarily gone from the childhood of Jesus to his passion, bypassing the whole public life. There is rich matter here for

rosary meditation, such as the wedding feast of Cana, and incidents from the public life where Mary's presence and Mary's name serve as occasions for her Son to give us a lesson in discipleship: "Still more blessed are they who hear the word of God and keep it" (Lk 11:28). Rosary vigils have already been introduced in some places, with an instructive use of readings, from Old Testament as well as New, and with recitation of a decade or two, if not all five. In a public celebration of the rosary, hymns can be introduced as well, and time allowed for periods of silent prayer.[20]

It should be clear that devotions honoring Mary, the Mother of Jesus, have a strong, constant tradition in the Church and that the rosary has a unique place in this heritage. It also ought to be evident that here as elsewhere we have great freedom to discover the way of prayer, including Marian prayer, most comfortable and effective for us.

Helpful Resources

Behold Your Mother: Woman of Faith. National Conference of Catholic Bishops. United States Catholic Conference Publications Office, 1312 Massachusetts Avenue, N.W., Washington, D.C. 20005.

Devotion to the Blessed Virgin Mary. Pope Paul VI. United States Catholic Conference Publications Office, 1312 Massachusetts Avenue, N.W., Washington, D.C. 20005.

Pray the Rosary. Robert C. Broderick. The Leaflet Missal Company, 419 W. Minnehaha Avenue, St. Paul, Minnesota 55103.

Scriptural Rosary. Christianica Center, 6 North Michigan Avenue, Chicago, Illinois 60602.

◇ *Method #2:*

The Church's Official Prayer Book

All of the ritual books revised since and according to the Second Vatican Council contain preliminary introduction or instruction sections which are rich in both doctrinal teaching and pastoral suggestions.

Thus, for example, each of the texts which provide us with our current official Roman Catholic rites for Mass, baptism, penance, anointing of the sick and funerals includes a General Introduction or General Instruction preceding the actual ceremonial regulations, prayers, readings and blessings.

So, too, the Church's official prayer book, formerly termed the Divine Office or Breviary and now named the Liturgy of the Hours, includes its own remarkably profound, inspirational and wise General Instruction. The Appendix of *Behind Closed Doors* reproduces excerpts from that total text and I urge readers to study this entire document for several reasons.

First of all, it describes in detail the Liturgy of the Hours' external structure and content.

Second, it offers a wonderful, even if succinct treatment of prayer.

Third, it explains the theological reasons behind the Church's official prayer and why we should make it a part of our own prayer lives.

Fourth, it examines the Liturgy of the Hours' various elements, like the Psalms, biblical readings, singing and silence, showing their great value for a person's spirituality and how we can integrate them into our patterns of prayer.

I have read the General Instruction several times, but the other night in preparation for writing this section I went through the entire text again at a single sitting. Its wealth of information and inspiration impressed me once more and confirmed my decision to include it here.

Nevertheless, those unfamiliar with this prayer form may find parts of the General Instruction at first glance technical and confusing. Therefore, I would recommend that such individuals initially read over the total instruction lightly, swiftly and easily. In that process they should simply catch the overall thrust of the document, note its major divisions and identify the portions which seem to concentrate on the theology or spirituality of the Hours and those which attend to the mechanics of how to recite or sing the Hours.

After this relatively quick glimpse, the neophyte could then return repeatedly and study small portions of those theological or spiritual sections. That bit by bit, day by day savoring of the General Instruction, similar to the approach urged for *Behind Closed Doors*, will supply real nourishment and guidance in an on-going way for the concerned Christian. Moreover, it could provide over a lengthy period of time a regular source of ideas and motivation for one's daily prayer period.

If the reader already prays often the Liturgy of the Hours or contemplates doing so in the future, the more technical or mechanical sections obviously will prove valuable. For the beginner, we will discuss some practical ways of starting or introducing the Liturgy of the Hours on a personal or parish basis in the last part of this chapter. However, let me say that normally speaking we can more easily learn how to use this excellent but complex prayer book through the personal guidance of a veteran than by private study, however careful, of the directions found in the General Instruction.

It would be repetitious for me in this chapter merely to summarize or restate the content of the General Instruction. Instead I will sketch the development of the Church's official prayer, suggest reasons why the Liturgy of the Hours could be profitable for us, and propose pragmatic measures for incorporating this prayer form into our lives.

How the Liturgy of the Hours Developed

Psalm 119:164 reads: "Seven times a day I praise you for your just ordinances." The term "seven" indicates, as it often does in the Old Testament or Hebrew Scriptures, an indefinite number of times.[1] On the other hand, over the years some have seen this as at least a partial inspiration behind the Divine Office which, in its pre-Vatican II version, seemed to summon a person seven times daily for formal prayer.

An examination of Scripture and an understanding of Jewish culture during the period of the early Church indicates how the first Christians individually and in groups prayed throughout the day at specified times.

We have already seen in Part I the excerpt from Acts 2:42–47 describing the communal life of the infant Church. "They went to the temple area together every day . . . " and "With exultant and sincere hearts they took their meals in common, praising God . . . "

Very soon during those formative years it became standard practice to pray alone or together at dusk when the sun went down and the evening lamps were lighted. Similarly, at dawn when the rising sun started to dispel darkness, the Christian community assembled for prayer. All of the natural images surrounding those movements, e.g., darkness and light, dying and rising, end and beginning, found their way into the formal prayers and took on rich symbolic meanings which carry over even today in our contemporary worship formulas.

The Christians also prayed at determined occasions throughout the day.

The Jewish people computed time from sunup to sundown. Thus, the first hour was 6:00 A.M; the third, 9:00 A.M.; the sixth, 12:00 noon; the ninth, 3:00 P.M.; the twelfth, 6:00 P.M. Older versions of the Bible translate times literally while newer ones adjust the original practice to our current computations. An awareness of this earlier concept, however, will make clearer the designations of sections of the pre-Vatican II Divine Office, as we shall see shortly.

To illustrate: On Pentecost the Christians were "all together in one place" praying when the Holy Spirit descended and filled them with the remarkable power of speaking in tongues. Some thought these people acting and talking so strangely had imbibed too much alcohol. Peter, standing up with the Eleven, spoke out to the critics, "These men are not drunk, as you suppose, for it is only the third hour of the day" (Acts 2:1, 14–15).

This particular translation, known as the Confraternity of Christian Doctrine version, dates back to 1941. In seeking for such an older text, I just looked through one bookcase and discovered a badly battered volume with my name on the title page and these words, "29 November 1948, Notre Dame, Indiana." I must also confess that crossed out above my name was this inscription, "Forrest J. Stephens, Freshman—Sept. '46—Commerce." Obviously neither one of us had a terribly high appreciation of Scripture in those far away years—he selling the book to a lowly underclassman and I content to purchase a second-hand copy of the good news. It did amaze and amuse me, however, to notice how I had underlined certain verses, even using two colors, and made marginal notes throughout the entire New Testament. That, no doubt, occurred in subsequent seminary days.[2] Please excuse the nostalgic diversion.

On the other hand, *The New American Bible* version of 1970 which we have been employing throughout this book translates those same passages: "When the day of Pentecost came it found them in one place . . . . Peter stood up with the Eleven, raised his voice, and addressed them . . . . You must realize that these men are not drunk, as you seem to think. It is only nine in the morning."

The point, of course, is that at the third hour or 9:00 A.M., the first Christians had assembled as a body for prayer.

Later on in Acts, we read: "About noontime the next day, as the men were traveling along and approaching the city, Peter went up to the roof terrace to pray" (Acts 10:9). The 1941 translation has it, "Peter went up to the roof to pray, about the sixth hour."

On another occasion we note, "Once, when Peter and John

were going up to the temple for prayer at the three o'clock hour
. . . " (Acts 3:1). The older translation reads, "Now Peter and
John were going up into the temple at the ninth hour of prayer."

We also observe how Paul and his companion prayed in jail
during the middle of the night. "About midnight, while Paul and
Silas were praying and singing hymns to God as their fellow prisoners listened . . . " (Acts 16:25).

In our discussion on the rosary, we commented on the tradition, especially in monasteries, of religious reciting or singing
daily or according to a determined schedule the 150 Psalms.

Over the centuries that custom of sanctifying the day through
prayer at regular and specified periods became more formalized in
its content and organized according to time. This prayer came to
be known as the Liturgy of the Hours (the present title) or the Divine Office (indicating that the praise of God is a duty we must discharge) or the Breviary (because of the abbreviated book
employed by the clergy for its recitation).[3]

The last two titles leave something to be desired.

The "Divine Office" rightly conveys the notion of our obligation to give praise and glory to God. However, we also do that in
the Eucharist or Mass. Consequently, "Divine Office" lacks a bit
of clarity.

The "Breviary" refers to the reduced size book or books containing the Psalms, readings and prayers of the Divine Office used
mostly in former days by clergy in the active pastoral ministry.
However, the Liturgy of the Hours is an action of praise by people, not a book. We do not, in similar fashion, say that the priest
will now pray the Missal when about to offer Mass. So, too, it is
inappropriate to state that we pray the Breviary. Moreover, that
older notion of the Breviary merely reinforced the notion that only
priests (the then known clergy) recited or sang the Church's official prayer.

The phrase or title Liturgy of the Hours, therefore, better
conveys the true notion of the Church's official prayer of praise by
which we sanctify the hours of each day.

Tracing the complete and complex historical development of
the formalized Liturgy of the Hours would naturally require a

good bit of space and not greatly serve the purpose of this book. Here I wish only to outline the format generally followed in the decades immediately before the Second Vatican Council and used normally by priests in pastoral ministry.

◇ We read from a multi-volume set, "the Breviary" which contained the entire text in Latin.

◇ All 150 Psalms were recited or sung each week.

◇ Most priests took their obligation to "read the breviary" very conscientiously, often staying up late and struggling in their weariness to complete the hour-long task of recitation before midnight.

◇ Few lay persons prayed the full Divine Office, although some did possess shortened and modified versions, using them daily or occasionally.

◇ There were eight parts: Matins (now the Office of Readings), Lauds (today's Morning Prayer), Prime (First hour or 6:00 A.M.), Terce (Third hour or 9:00 A.M.), Sext (Sixth hour or 12 noon), None (Ninth hour or 3:00 P.M.), Vespers (now Evening Prayer) and Compline (today's Night Prayer). Since Matins often was combined with Lauds or anticipated the night before and also had more the character of spiritual nourishment for us through various readings than of pure praise of God, we could see the others combining to become the "seven times a day I praise you for your just ordinances."

◇ Instead of reciting these at the appropriate moments throughout the day, the clergy often read the total breviary at one sitting, preferably early in the day. Some books on spirituality for priests actually recommended this "safe" practice. In that way there was no danger that because of human weakness and unforeseen pastoral demands they might fail to discharge such a serious duty.

◇ Priests usually prayed the Breviary alone and were supposed to move their lips even when reciting the texts by themselves. Older Catholics certainly have memories of clergy pacing back and forth beside church or rectory quite intent on a small, but thick, soft leather bound black book and with lips moving silently in prayer.

The Second Vatican Council Fathers decreed the revision of the Divine Office just as they ordered the reform of all the other liturgical books.[4] Some of the major modifications, ordered then and to be found today in the renewed Liturgy of the Hours, are:

◇ The sequence of the hours has been restored so they more easily can be recited daily at the proper time and thus fulfill their purpose of sanctifying the day.

◇ Lauds becomes Morning Prayer and Vespers becomes Evening Prayer, with both termed the chief hours and the two hinges on which the daily office turns.

◇ Compline is changed to Night Prayer and revised so as suitably to mark the day's close.

◇ Matins, now the Office of Readings, contains fewer psalms, longer readings and may be recited at any hour of the day or evening before.

◇ The hour of Prime has been dropped.

◇ The minor hours of Terce, Sext and None have been combined into Daytime Prayer with a mid-morning, mid-day or mid-afternoon component. Outside monastic or choral recitation, we select the one most suited to the time of day.

◇ The 150 Psalms have been distributed over a four week cycle with a few difficult psalms and some awkward verses omitted.

◇ The clergy are encouraged to pray the Liturgy of the Hours together when feasible.

◇ "The laity, too, are encouraged to recite the Divine Office, either with the priests, or among themselves, or even individually."

English translations of the revised Liturgy of the Hours are available in various formats. Four volume sets contain the entire texts and will cost between $75 and $100; single bound volumes with complete Morning and Evening Prayer can be purchased for $15 to $20; various paperbacks or pamphlets with selected excerpts from the official text suitable for group or individual prayer are available for a few dollars each.

Catholic bookshops normally carry a stock of these different type publications.

Reasons for Praying the Liturgy of the Hours

St. Ignatius Loyola said in the "Foundations" of his *Spiritual Exercises*, "Humans were created to praise, venerate and serve the Lord their God, and in that way to save their souls."[5]

The Liturgy of the Hours is essentially that kind of praise, a biblically based prayer in which we as individuals, yet more, as part of the Church, honor, glorify and adore the Lord.

In the Constitution on the Sacred Liturgy, the Council fathers viewed the Liturgy of the Hours as essentially a song or hymn of praise.

Jesus Christ, high priest of the new and eternal covenant, taking human nature, introduced into this earthly exile that hymn which is sung throughout all ages in the halls of heaven. He attaches to himself the entire community of mankind and has them join him in singing his divine song of praise.

For he continues his priestly work through his Church. The Church, by celebrating the Eucharist and by other means, especially the celebration of the Divine Office, is ceaselessly engaged in praising the Lord and interceding for the salvation of the entire world.

The Divine Office, in keeping with ancient Christian tradition, is so devised that the whole course of the day and night is made holy by the praise of God. Therefore, when this wonderful song of praise is correctly celebrated by priests and others deputed to it by the Church, or by the faithful praying together with a priest in the approved form, then it is truly the voice of the Bride herself addressed to her Bridegroom. It is the very prayer which Christ himself together with his body addresses to the Father.

Hence all who take part in the Divine Office are not only performing a duty for the Church, they are also sharing in what is the greatest honor for Christ's bride; for by offering these praises to God they are standing before God's throne in the name of the Church, their Mother.

Priests who are engaged in the sacred pastoral ministry will pray the Divine Office the more fervently, the more alive they are to the need to heed St. Paul's exhortation, "Pray without ceasing" (1 Thes 5:17). For only the Lord, who said, "Without me you can do nothing," can make their work effective and fruitful. That is why the apostles when instituting deacons said, "We will devote ourselves to prayer and to the ministry of the word" (Acts 6:4).[6]

We summarize below some of the reasons for praying the Liturgy of the Hours.

It is the *prayer of Christ*. Since the Church is the body of Christ intimately linked with the Savior, we the members cannot be cut off from our Lord, the head. Thus, in the ancient words of St. Augustine, "When we, the body of the Son, pray, the head is not separate from the body. It is our Lord Jesus Christ, the one Savior of his own body, who prays for us, who prays in us and to whom we pray."

It is the *prayer of the Church*. When we pray the Liturgy of the Hours, we do so not alone, not as isolated individuals, nor as a solitary group, but united with the whole Church militant, suffering and triumphant. That is, we join our voices in praise with living members throughout the world, with those suffering in purgatory and with the saints in heaven.

It is a *biblical prayer*. Each of the hours contains Psalms, readings from the Scriptures and other texts that are either excerpts from the Bible or heavily biblical in content. Our prayer thus is largely articulated in words inspired by the Holy Spirit.

It is a *prayer of the heart*. Psalms make up the major portion of any hour. Those God-given songs of praise echo the deepest sentiments of the human heart—e.g. joy, sorrow, anxiety, gratitude, repentance. Regular use of them through the Liturgy of the Hours can help place our inner concerns in a divine context and allow the Lord to surround them with light.

It is a *prayer for others*. Whether recited privately or prayed communally, the Liturgy of the Hours speaks to God about the needs of the whole Church and the entire human race. In the words of the General Instruction for the text, a person "is praying in the name of the Church and . . . can therefore find in the name of the Church constant cause for joy and sorrow."

Thus we may as individuals be sad and the psalm be joyful or feel elated and the psalm express distress. However, in the

Church throughout the world someone or some group of people are experiencing the sentiments contained in the Psalm. If we raise our thoughts to those rejoicing or grieving people it gives meaning to our praying the Psalm when our own mood seems quite the opposite from the tone of the assigned Psalm.

In St. Paul's words we in this fashion, "Rejoice with those who are glad, and mourn with those in sorrow" (Romans 12:15).

Careful, prayerful reflection on the spiritual or theological portions of the General Instruction in the Appendix will expand upon and deepen the values or benefits of the Liturgy of the Hours expressed here.

Some Practical Suggestions for Using the Liturgy of the Hours

◊ *Parish Celebrations of Morning and/or Evening Prayer*

The Constitution on the Liturgy urged this in its suggestions for revision of the Divine Office. "Pastors of souls should see to it that the principal hours, especially Vespers, are celebrated in common in church on Sundays and on the more solemn feasts."

The General Instruction naturally follows through with that recommendation. Article 21 reads:

> Whenever possible, other groups of the faithful should come together in church to celebrate the principal hours of the liturgy. The most important of these groups are the local parishes—the cells of the diocese—established under the leadership of a pastor who takes the place of the bishop. Since parishes "in a certain way represent the visible Church as it is established throughout the world," they should celebrate the principal hours publicly in church whenever it is possible.

While there has not been widespread implementation of this ideal, more and more parishes do offer a public celebration of Evening Prayer or Vespers on the Sundays of Advent or Lent. Some parishes celebrate these hours fifteen minutes before a morning or afternoon Mass. The Rochester diocese used a regional celebration of Evening Prayer during the weekdays of one Lent as the format for a communal worship event gathering many parishes around the bishop on the occasion of his visit to each area.

◊ *Integrating Morning and/or Evening Prayer with Mass*
Section VII in Chapter II of the General Instruction specifically mentions "Joining the Hours of the Liturgy with Mass or with Other Hours."

I had personal experience for a half dozen years with that practice as pastor of Holy Family Church in Fulton, New York. With a $300 donation from one parishioner we purchased twenty copies of *Christian Prayer* and began on a regular basis to integrate Morning Prayer with our 9:15 A.M. Mass and Evening Prayer with our 5:15 P.M. Eucharist.

The format is relatively simple.

After an opening song, reverence to the altar and greeting of the people, the priest invites the congregation to pray with him the three Psalms of Morning or Evening Prayer. The presider then offers the opening prayer of Mass.

The readings are taken from the day's Mass followed by a brief homily and concluded with the Prayer of the Faithful or General Intercessions as found in the Liturgy of the Hours.

Mass continues with the presentation of the gifts. After Communion, priest and congregation pray the canticle of Zechariah from Luke 1:68–79 (Morning Prayer) or Mary from Luke 1:46–55 (Evening Prayer) with its appropriate antiphon.

The presider offers the Prayer after Communion and ends Mass in the usual way.

We found that this procedure enriched weekday Eucharists, did not require that much extra time and received positive acceptance by the ten to thirty daily Mass-goers.

◊ *Part of Parish Council Sessions*
Our Syracuse diocesan guidelines for parish councils suggest that members set aside fifteen minutes for prayer at the start of each session. The Liturgy of the Hours provides a rich, varied and ready resource for that introductory segment of the meeting.

St. Michael's Church in Central Square, New York uses the bound volume of *Christian Prayer* for Evening Prayer on those occasions. St. Mary's Church in Jamesville, New York employs a less expensive, but less complete pamphlet, "Praying with Christ" in the same way.

◇ *As Introductory Prayer for Church Meetings*

Following the same approach, many parish staffs use the Liturgy of the Hours—Morning, Daytime or Evening Prayer depending upon the time of day—to begin their deliberations in a prayerful way. In similar fashion our diocesan administrative cabinet which meets every few weeks with the bishop generally turns to the Liturgy of the Hours for a prayer to start its sessions.

◇ *Expressions of the Human Heart*

Psalms make up the major portion of the Liturgy of the Hours. Those inspired songs, as mentioned above, echo the deepest feelings of the human heart and our inner selves—hope, discouragement, joy, sorrow, remorse, gratitude, praise, need. Prayerful recitation, singing and pondering of the Psalms on a regular basis facilitates expression of these intimate sentiments. It also will help us better understand and more sensitively appreciate their presence within ourselves and in others. Chapter III, Section I on "The Psalms and Their Close Relationship with Christian Prayer" in the General Instruction contains a superb treatment of this very topic. Further study of the Psalms obviously will prove valuable.

◇ *Prayer for the Wider World*

We all have an inherent inclination to be self-centered in our prayer. What is happening within me and to those who immediately surround or touch my life tends to occupy my interest. While those are all legitimate concerns for prayer, we as humans, Christians and members of the Church need also to reach out prayerfully toward our sisters and brothers in the wider world. Their joys and sorrows, hopes and fears, victories and defeats should be ours as well.

Understanding the Liturgy of the Hours as the prayer of the universal Church can help in this regard. Article 108 of the General Instruction offers insight on that point, specifically in relation to the Psalms.

The daily paper, Catholic press, and radio or television news, together with our everyday contacts, provide us with an ever fresh source of people and situations needing our prayer. Mary just had a baby; Sam undergoes surgery tomorrow; the Pope is traveling to another country; a bitter strike continues; an alienated Catholic returns to the Church; a plane crashes; farmers need rain; several adults receive baptism, confirmation and Eucharist on Holy Saturday; my mother is dying; our son passed his law examination.

With those thoughts stretching our minds and interests as we pray, the Church's prayer, including the Psalms, will have additional meaning.

◇ *Simple Beginnings*

Here we are at the end of this chapter, and let us presume that you have never before heard of, much less prayed, the Liturgy of the Hours. Certain obvious questions thus arise. How do I start? Where do we begin? What books are available? I offer these suggestions:

1. Start slowly.
2. Read the Appendix as recommended, concentrating on the theological and spiritual portions and gliding over for now the more technical "how to" sections.
3. Invest in one of the cheaper publications cited below.
4. Pray a section each day, aware of the ideas sketched in this chapter and the General Instruction.
5. When you are comfortable with this prayer and have become convinced it has value for your own prayer life, move up the ladder and purchase *Christian Prayer* with the complete Morning and Evening Prayer for each day.
6. If you become, then, truly excited by this method, save your money and obtain for about $100 the four volume *Liturgy of the Hours* containing the total Divine Office. That is the Church's complete official prayer book.

Helpful Resources

Praying with Christ. The Liturgical Press, Collegeville, Minnesota. A booklet for about $2.00 containing excerpts from the Liturgy of the Hours. Good for the introductory steps.

Night Prayer. United States Catholic Conference, Publications Office, 1312 Massachusetts Avenue, N.W., Washington, D.C. 20005. A booklet available for about $2.00 with night prayer for each evening of the week. Good for the bedside.

Daytime Prayer. United States Catholic Conference, Publications Office at the above address. A paperback around $5.00 which could be helpful for prayer at the start of meetings.

Morning and Evening Prayer. Regina Press, New York and Liturgical Press, Collegeville, Minnesota. Paperbound book between $5.00 and $10.00 with selected Morning and Evening Prayer and some music.

Christian Prayer. Catholic Book Publishing Company, Daughters of St. Paul, Helicon Press, Liturgical Press. Hardcover book between $10.00 and $20.00 containing full Morning and Evening Prayer plus other excerpts and music.

Liturgy of the Hours. Catholic Book Publishing Co. Leather cover, four volume set with entire *Liturgy of the Hours* costing between $75.00 and $100.00.

The Liturgy of the Hours. A.M. Roguet, O.P., The Liturgical Press, Collegeville, Minnesota. A $4.95 paperback containing a commentary on the Liturgy of the Hours by one of the consultants to the Vatican for the revision of the Divine Office.

The Psalms. Carroll Stuhlmueller, C.P., Michael Glazier, Inc., 1723 Delaware Ave., Wilmington, Delaware 19806. Two volumes, large permanent paperback: I—Psalms 1–72, $9.95; II—Psalms 73–150, $8.95. Commentaries by a well respected Scripture scholar.

Suggested order for beginners: 1. *Praying with Christ* or *Night Prayer*; 2. *Morning and Evening Prayer*; 3. *Christian Prayer*.

◇ *Method #3:*

Reflective Biblical Reading

The comparative brevity of this chapter in no way indicates that reflective biblical reading is of less value or less desirable as a style of prayer than, for example, the rosary, Liturgy of the Hours, meditation or centering prayer. Quite the contrary, it may well be the best method with which to start, the easiest to sustain and the seemingly richest form of prayer we use.

The most appealing reason for this method, of course, rests upon the divine inspiration of the Bible. We read or hear in the Scriptures not merely human phrases, but God's words which have special power and meaning for us.

The Vatican Council fathers in the Dogmatic Constitution on Divine Revelation clearly taught the inspired authorship of the Sacred Scriptures:

> For Holy Mother Church, relying on the faith of the apostolic age, accepts as sacred and canonical the books of the Old and the New Testaments, whole and entire, with all their parts, on the grounds that, written under the inspiration of the Holy Spirit (cf. Jn 20:31; 2 Tim 3:16; 2 Pet 1:19–21; 3:15–16), they have God as their author and have been handed on as such to the Church itself.
>
> Since, therefore, all that the inspired authors, or sacred writers, affirm should be regarded as affirmed by the Holy Spirit, we must acknowledge that the books of Scripture, firmly, faithfully and without error, teach that truth which God, for the sake of our salvation, wished to see confided to the Sacred Scriptures. Thus "all Scripture is inspired by God, and profitable for teaching, for reproof, for correction and for training in righteousness, so that the man of God may be complete, equipped for every good work" (2 Tim 3:16–17, Gk. text).[1]

115

Given the divine dignity of the Bible, it was natural and logical for the bishops later in this same document to urge the clergy and others who engage in teaching God's Word to "immerse themselves in the Scriptures by constant sacred reading and diligent study."

> Therefore, all clerics, particularly priests of Christ and others who, as deacons or catechists, are officially engaged in the ministry of the Word, should immerse themselves in the Scriptures by constant sacred reading and diligent study. For it must not happen that anyone becomes "an empty preacher of the Word of God to others, not being a hearer of the Word in his own heart," when he ought to be sharing the boundless riches of the divine Word with the faithful committed to his care, especially in the sacred liturgy.[2]

However, the Council fathers also encouraged all followers of Christ, including the laity, frequently to read and pray the Scriptures:

> Likewise, the Sacred Synod forcefully and specifically exhorts all the Christian faithful, especially those who live the religious life, to learn "the surpassing knowledge of Jesus Christ" (Phil 3:8) by frequent reading of the divine Scriptures. "Ignorance of the Scriptures is ignorance of Christ." Therefore, let them go gladly to the sacred text itself, whether in the sacred liturgy, which is full of the divine words, or in devout reading, or in such suitable exercises and various other helps which, with the approval and guidance of the pastors of the Church, are happily spreading everywhere in our day. Let them remember, however, that prayer should accompany the reading of Sacred Scripture, so that a dialogue takes place between God and man. For, "we speak to him when we pray; we listen to him when we read the divine oracles."[3]

In the guidelines for the reform of the liturgy, the Council fathers hoped that we would recover, retain or deepen a "sweet and living love for Sacred Scripture."[4] This warm, respectful and yearning attitude toward the Bible can be manifested in many ways.

◊ *"By frequent reading of the divine Scriptures."*

In a subsequent section I will mention the story of my priest friend who began nearly ten years ago a more intense life of prayer after his Marriage Encounter experience. That greater concern about his inner needs eventually led him to a daily period of spiritual reading. I have watched him on vacation set a pocket calculator alarm clock for 15 minutes, take up his Bible and spend that time in prayerful reading of God's Word.

Consistency and persistence are the key ingredients of this virtuous habit. The person who day after day sets a quarter of an hour for the inspired text will be surprised just how much of the Bible she or he covers in the course of a year. My friend, by his diligent observance of the practice, has already read through twice the entire Old and New Testaments.

George Martin has written a most helpful paperback on this topic entitled, *Reading Scripture as the Word of God.* In it he suggests fifteen minutes a day for such reading and then explains the reason for that particular amount of time: "Five minutes is too little to really immerse oneself in the Word of God; a half an hour is too long for most of us to sustain an alert and prayerful reading of Scripture, at least at the beginning."[5]

He envisions these fifteen minutes spent in "sustained, reflective reading, alert to both detail and context, which gradually draws us deeper into the mystery of God's revelation in Scripture."[6]

That type of reading is distinct from several other ways of approaching the Bible: a rapid covering of a whole book or section, an intense meditation on a single verse, a thorough study of a passage or the reflective prayer I will describe at the end of this chapter.

Martin explains his recommendation of a method for the fifteen minute, daily reading of the Bible:

> Between the sustained reading of a long passage or entire books of Scripture and intensive reflection on a few words lies the kind of reading that should form the basis of our daily reading of Scripture. This reading is characterized neither by a desire to cover a certain amount of material, nor by an attempt to

milk the last ounce of meaning from every single verse. It is careful reading, with pauses to reflect on the meaning of what is being read. It is slow reading, leisurely reading, reading with attention to detail and nuance. It is reading with a deliberate yet natural pace, that allows us to linger over a single striking verse or thought before continuing on.[7]

◊ *By "diligent study" of the Bible.*

If we truly care about someone or something, we normally wish to know as much as possible about the individual or the subject. As a too avid sports fan, for example, I can devour when available *The Sporting News*, carefully noting all the statistics about the players of my favorite baseball team. Not only do I study the facts concerning those on the Philadelphia Phillies' major league roster, but I also examine every detail printed about their future stars now on some minor league team in Portland, Oregon, Reading, Pennsylvania or Spartanburg, South Carolina.

In similar fashion, if I really love the Lord and the words God has communicated to us, I will want to extract as much meaning as possible from the inspired text. That means a diligent, on-going study of the Scriptures.

There are several rather simple and easy ways for the non-scholar to carry on this study.

First, by reading through rather swiftly a whole book or long section to get an overview of it. Martin explains the purpose and value of such a quick journey through the biblical text.

> It is profitable, for instance, to read some of Paul's shorter letters as we would read any letter we receive: reading it through from beginning to end, and then going back through it more slowly a second time. This type of rather quick reading is also appropriate for many parts of the Old Testament, particularly the historical books. A straight-through reading of a long section provides an idea of "the lay of the land"; the more significant passages can be marked for later careful reading and reflection.[8]

Second, by examining the footnotes in a substantial version like the *New American Bible* and *Jerusalem Bible*.

Third, by reading the introduction to a particular book of the Bible.

Fourth, by noting the cross-references of a verse or section and looking them up. It is fascinating, for example, to compare the various accounts of the transfiguration or calming of the sea; it is equally engaging to observe the roots of a New Testament saying in the Old Testament or Hebrew Scriptures.

Fifth, by obtaining a respected, readable commentary and faithfully moving through it much as we would the daily reading of the Bible itself. I list two of these well regarded commentaries at the end of this chapter.

◊ *By an attitude which prompts us to "listen to him," to Christ who challenges us when we read the Bible or hear the Scriptures proclaimed.*

God's Word and Jesus' teaching is indeed good news, offering us forgiveness, strength, wisdom and salvation. But the inspired message, like an effective homily or sermon, also will or should unsettle us. We discover, after reflection upon the divine message, that some patterns of acting or thinking in our lives require change. Such a call to conversion will always cause a little or a lot of pain and we can expect to experience some defensive, resisting feelings or thoughts as the summons to repent and alter our style of living makes its voice heard within us.

St. Monica's son, Augustine, went through that very process of a biblically inspired conversion. In his youth the brilliant lad strayed from the path of truth and tasted recklessly and to the full the pleasures this world offers which included the fathering of a child without benefit of marriage.

His mother's almost twenty years of prayer and fasting for him together with his discovery of this life's ultimately unsatisfying quality ("Lord, you have made us for yourself, and we will be restless until we rest in you") led Augustine to seek baptism in 387 from St. Ambrose, the bishop of Milan.

Just prior to that positive step or choice in his life, however, while wrestling with the Lord in prayer and trying to discern the direction he should take, Augustine heard a child's voice singing out, "Take it and read it. Take it and read it." *Tolle et lege* is the famous Latin text for that injunction. He describes what happened next in his *Confessions.*

> I checked the force of my tears and rose to my feet, being quite certain that I must interpret this as a divine command to me to open the Bible and read the first passage which I should come upon. For I had heard this about St. Anthony: he had happened to come in when the Gospel was being read, and as though the words read were spoken directly to himself had received the admonition: "Go, sell all that you have, and give to the poor, and you shall have treasure in heaven, and come and follow me." And by such a message he had been immediately converted.
>
> I snatched up the Bible, opened it, and read in silence the passage upon which my eyes first fell: "Not in reveling and drunkeness, not in debauchery and licentiousness, not in quarreling and jealousy. But put on the Lord Jesus Christ, and make no provision for the flesh, to gratify its desires." I had no wish to read further; there was no need to. For immediately I had reached the end of this sentence it was as though my heart was filled with a light of confidence and all the shadows of my doubt were swept away (Book VIII, Chapter 12).[9]

◇ *By using the "boundless riches of the divine Word" as a resource for meditation.*

In the next chapter we will describe a specific method of reflective prayer commonly called meditation. There we will also note some published resources which list biblical passages particularly suitable for this type of prayer. Finally, in that section I will outline a process of preparation using the Bible itself or the sacred liturgy, "which is full of the divine words," as the start-up point for the next day's meditative reflection.

◇ *By putting the inspired texts on our lips or in our hearts as we "speak to God when we pray."*

As we mentioned in the previous chapter, the Psalms echo the deepest sentiments of the human heart. They also, obviously, are part of the Bible and thus inspired phrases. Consequently, when we recite or sing them or employ them in silent, personal prayer, we are speaking to God with God's own words, a concept that is especially powerful.

There are, nevertheless, many other portions of the Bible besides the Psalms which could be used to articulate our prayerful inner sentiments. Part I of this book contained many samples of such scriptural texts—for example, "Speak, for your servant is listening" (1 Samuel 3:10), or "Increase our faith" (Luke 17:5).

A perhaps often untapped source of those biblical phrases is the Book of Revelation. Sprinkled throughout that often enigmatic work are hymns of praise which can serve exceptionally well as words to express our interior movements of adoration and thanksgiving.

Here are three samples:

"Holy, holy, holy, is the Lord God Almighty . . . " (Revelation 4:8).

"O Lord our God, you are worthy to receive glory and honor and power! For you have created all things; by your will they came to be and were made" (Revelation 4:11).

"Worthy is the lamb that was slain to receive power and riches, wisdom and strength, honor and glory and praise" (Revelation 5:12).

◇ *By reflective biblical reading as a prayerful "dialogue" with God.*

This is the reflective biblical reading which I would term a specific method of praying. It differs from careful study of the Bible, the daily fifteen minute reading of the Scriptures, an intense examination of one word or phrase, meditation on a passage or even using phrases like the Psalms or a text from Revelation for prayer.

Reflective biblical reading is extremely simple, easy to begin or continue, scripturally rich, of course, and especially helpful when we feel fatigued or preoccupied with other concerns.

It works in this way:

1. Use the regular prayer time as described in Part I with the location, the set aside moments and the preparation as noted there.

2. Once seated and settled, take the Bible in hand and for a moment or two be conscious that this is a holy book, these are God-inspired words, and the Lord is speaking to you.

3. Briefly ask the Holy Spirit to open your eyes, mind and heart to the text before you. That can be a spontaneous prayer or a formal one normally included in most Bibles.

4. Open up the Bible to a random spot or to a previously selected passage. Read the section through somewhat slowly and easily to catch the flavor and overall content.

5. Return to the beginning and read very slowly and prayerfully, aware that God is speaking to you, that you are listening and that you may respond as the Spirit prompts. As soon as a word, phrase or sentence seems to have a certain richness or power for you, stop and turn it over and over within your mind and heart. Taste, relish, devour the passage. Allow any interior aspirations which arise to surface.

6. When that word, phrase or sentence begins to lose its richness or power, gently move on and repeat the process. Continue until your prayer time has expired.

7. At the end, draw the period together with an explicit act of gratitude, faith and petition for that opportunity to experience God's Word.

On some occasions you may never get beyond a word or a phrase. It seems so rich that there is no desire to move ahead. On other days, no word or phrase inspires and you merely keep reading along, even if slowly and reflectively. Those occasions, much like prayer at moments of dryness or darkness, may feel unsatisfying and appear unproductive. In God's sight, however, the very opposite could be true. Persevering with such reflective biblical reading during arid or dark periods requires faith and love. It means that we are speaking to God even if our senses say God isn't talking to us today. The fact is that the Lord probably touches, informs and fills our inner selves more on those days than on days of greater tangible consolations.

Helpful Resources

Reading Scripture as the Word of God. George Martin. Servant Books, Dept. 200, Box 7455, Ann Arbor, Michigan 48107 ($4.95). A most useful, easy to read, up to date paperback on this topic.

The Collegeville Bible Commentary. Liturgical Press, St. John's Abbey, Collegeville, Minnesota 56321. A popular Catholic commentary by good scholars in eleven volumes which includes the New American Bible translation. Attractive, illustrated paperback and reasonable ($2.50 each; $25.00 for eleven volume set).

The Daily Bible Series. William Barclay. The Westminster Press, Philadelphia. A popular, multi-volume paperback commentary on the New Testament by a well-known Protestant Scripture scholar. Richer and more detailed, but more expensive than the Collegeville version (eighteen volume set for $99.95; single volumes at $5.95).

◇ *Method #4:*

Meditation

Time magazine for June 6, 1983 carried a cover story on "Stress: Can We Cope?" Research scholars in this area, according to the article, have concluded that how one deals with life's trials and tribulations is more important for inner peace than the actual elimination or diminution of such difficulties.

Their studies also indicate that a curious blend of people are known to enjoy remarkably good health and longevity: Mormons, nuns, symphony conductors and women listed in *Who's Who.*[1]

They offer no clear or certain explanation of that phenomenon. However, later in the essay the authors cite some hard statistics by Harvard cardiologist Herbert Benson which show a direct connection between a regular pattern of personal meditation and positive physiological changes such as decreased heart rate, lower blood pressure and reduced oxygen consumption. This data indicates that meditation practiced ten to twenty minutes once or twice a day lessens stress-related symptoms and thus becomes a natural antidote to tension.[2]

While meditation does seem to possess great power for bringing peace into our hearts, calming our bodies and placing the events of our lives in proper perspective, those practical benefits for better living are not the only or even the main reasons why we encourage meditation. The meditation we describe in this chapter is a form of prayer, a method to help us be in God's presence, a particular way of speaking to God and listening to the Lord speak to us. Those anxiety-reducing, natural side-effects are welcomed, but we would and do meditate even if they do not seem to occur.

Meditation, as we will outline it, involves an active use of our interior powers—the imagination, memory, reason and will. During a meditative period we attempt, for example, to see Jesus in our mind, to hear within us his words, to think about the action or saying of Christ under consideration and to stimulate sentiments of the heart or will like praise, faith, love, gratitude, repentance and petition. We also, toward the end of our meditation, seek to apply the reflection in specific ways to our daily living.

While a kind of passive listening to God often develops in meditation and is encouraged, this form of mental prayer differs in that respect from the centering prayer explained in the last chapter of *Behind Closed Doors*. The latter involves repeated use of one word or phrase to facilitate a centering on the presence of God at the core of our inner self. We refrain in centering prayer from reasoning on a topic and gently but deliberately put aside images which may enter our memory or imagination during the reflective period. Meditation, on the other hand, engages as much as possible all these powers as a means of leading the person at prayer into union with God.

These general statements should become clearer as we sketch two meditation techniques proposed by contemporary writers and provide an illustrative sample of a meditation.

◊ J. Murray Elwood, former director of the Newman Center at the State University of New York, Oswego campus, wrote *A Month with Christ* as an easy to learn and practical "way to pray the Gospels." This paperback explains the system he proposes, and then gives thirty examples of it using excerpts from the Gospels.[3]

After stressing the essential importance of "warming up" through the kinds of preparation for prayer we have detailed earlier, Elwood suggests that we first read very slowly a scene from the Gospels. Then "we enter that scene, copy the original experience and make it a springboard to prayer by following these three simple steps."

1. **Christ in My Eyes**. "We paint a mental picture of the Gospel scene in our imagination, not only visually, but with all our senses and feelings—in 'living color.' . . . With the help of mental imagery, we begin our meditation by reliving the Gospel scene as if we were experiencing it for the very first time."

2. Christ in My Heart. "Then we reflect for a moment on the way Jesus spoke or acted in this Gospel . . . . We answer him in our own way, with our own words. We tell him of our needs, our fears, our failures and our love. We talk to Jesus as our best and dearest friend, from our heart."

3. Christ in My Hands. "The third step is to use our prayer to help us live more honest, more Christ-like lives. So before finishing our meditation we ask ourselves how this Gospel scene applies to real-life situations . . . . Our decision should flow out of the Gospel scene into a concrete action in our daily lives."

As a follow-up or prolongation of the prayer, Elwood recommends "a few words or a line from Scripture that is intended to be used as brief spontaneous prayer for spare moments during the day . . . to lift our hearts to the Lord and recall our good resolutions to live the Gospel in our daily lives."[4]

◇ Father Henri J.M. Nouwen, whom we have cited frequently throughout this book, believes that unless we set aside a certain place and time each day to do nothing else but pray, we can never expect our unceasing thought to become unceasing prayer.[5] However, Nouwen also proposes a "very simple discipline for contemplative prayer" which he has found personally helpful both for that set aside period of prayer and for living out the rest of his day.

I would like now to present with commentary his own method for contemplative prayer or meditation.[6]

1. Read every evening before going to sleep the readings of the next day's Eucharist with special attention to the Gospel.

During my pre-Vatican II seminary days and in the early years of priesthood, I heard the great liturgical pioneer, Monsignor Martin Hellriegel, repeatedly make the same suggestion, but from a different context. "Prepare the Mass texts the night before," he would urge in his strong, warm, German accent. That recommendation, as I soon learned, pays rich dividends. Besides providing a resource for meditation, it in an almost mysterious manner makes those biblical and liturgical passages come alive with special power at the next day's Mass.

A relatively inexpensive daily missal can be helpful in making this practice much easier to implement. Moreover, I would also suggest Father Leonard Foley's *Saint of the Day* as a companion volume. His brief life of the saint we celebrate can also provide a topic for meditation to replace, accompany or supplement the scriptural text.[7]

2. It is often helpful to take one sentence or word that offers special comfort and repeat it a few times so that, with that one sentence or word, the whole content can be brought to mind and allowed slowly to descend from the mind into the heart.

I have found this practice to be a powerful support in times of crisis. It is especially helpful during the night, when worries or anxieties may keep me awake and seduce me into idolatry. By remembering the Gospel story or any of the sayings of the Old or New Testament authors, I can create a safe mental home into which I can lead all my preoccupations and let them be transformed into quiet prayer.

We all have varying patterns of going to sleep. For some like myself there normally are only a few seconds between the time the head hits the pillow and sleep comes; others toss and turn or lie awake thinking for an extended period of time; still others tend to read, listen to a radio talk show or watch television until the drop off mood arrives. In all of these differing styles, however, there are normally some moments when we stay there with eyes closed waiting for the "letting go" of waking consciousness to occur.

Nouwen's recommendation about that biblical word, phrase or sentence—a suggestion I recall hearing in seminary training thirty years ago—contains several beneficial elements. Silently and easily repeating this key word or phrase over and over again as we await sleep can:

(a) quiet our troubled or over-active mind and actually help induce sleep (it certainly surpasses counting sheep);

(b) allow our subconscious self to work on those scriptural thoughts while we are resting;

(c) prevent inappropriate or undesirable images or thoughts from securing a firm hold on our mind and imagination during those vulnerable minutes;

(d) provide us upon arising with a readily recalled thought to lift our minds and hearts in prayer as we struggle to rise from the death of sleep and move rather semi-consciously through our "getting up and getting dressed routine";

(e) offer a quieting, inspirational thought should we awaken in the middle of the night.

3. **During the following day, a certain time must be set apart for explicit contemplation.**

We have spoken at length about this in Part I of *Behind Closed Doors*.

4. **This is a time in which to look at Christ as he appears in the reading. The best way to do this is to read the Gospel of the day again and to imagine the Lord as he speaks or acts with his people. In this hour we can see him, hear him, touch him, and make him present to our whole being. We can see Christ as our healer, our teacher, and our guide. We can see him in his indignation, in his compassion, in his suffering, and in his glory. We can look at him, listen to him, and enter into conversation with him.**

One can see in this a similarity with the *Christ in My Heart* step of J. Murray Elwood. That is the essence, the purpose of the prayer technique. It should lead us to the point where we are present with the Lord, both speaking and listening to God within us.

Here is likewise a most personal, intimate and varying moment for us. We are in conversation with Christ about the deepest concerns of our human hearts. At the same time, given our human condition, that exchange may sometimes be lively and satisfying, sometimes forced and frustrating, sometimes weary and distracting. There are also occasions when we either feel very inclined only to listen and be still or even experience a certain pain and discomfort if we try to speak, albeit silently, to the Lord. Those symptoms normally indicate that God wants us to remain quiet and attentive, hearing what the Spirit may be whispering within. Such receptive, passive and listening prayer should be highly valued and not swiftly judged as laziness and a waste.

5. **For me, this discipline of having an "empty time" just to be with Christ as he speaks to me in the readings of the day has proven very powerful. I have discovered that during the rest of the day, wherever I am or whatever I am doing, the image of Christ that I have contemplated during that "empty time" stays with me as a beautiful icon. Sometimes it is the conscious center of all my thoughts, but more often it is a quiet presence of which I am only indirectly aware. In the beginning I hardly noticed the difference. Slowly, however, I realized that I could carry Christ, the image of God, with me and let him affect not only my reflective thoughts but my daydreams as well. I am even convinced that this simple form of daily contemplation will eventually make my dreams again gateways of God's on-going revelation.**

Again we note a parallel with Elwood's *Christ in My Hands.*

6. **Finally, this discipline puts the celebration of the Eucharist into a totally new perspective. Especially when it is celebrated in the evening, the Eucharist becomes a real climax in which the Lord with whom we have journeyed during the day speaks to us again in the context of the whole community and invites us with our friends into the intimacy of his table. It is there that the transformation of all images into the image of Christ finds its fullest realization. It is there that the unity with Christ experienced through contemplation finds its perfection. Daily contemplation makes the daily Eucharist a transforming celebration. When we live the whole day with**

Christ in mind and heart, the Eucharist can never be merely a routine or an obligation. Instead it becomes the center of daily life toward which everything is directed.

The above observation reinforces a point Father Nouwen has made in other writings—the centrality of the daily Eucharist in his own life. We therefore can see that for him his regular hour of prayer leads into and flows out of holy Mass.

◊ I would like now to illustrate the basic notion of meditation according to the steps above. To do so I will use as the resource text an incident in which Jesus, asleep in a boat with the apostles, was awakened, then miraculously calmed the wind and stilled the Sea of Galilee. That calming of the storm occurs in each of the Synoptic Gospels: Matthew 8:23–27; Mark 4:35–41; Luke 8:22–25.

1. The night before, we read the story over either in a simple way or in a more thorough, studious manner.

Following the simpler procedure, we examine only one account, say Mark 4:35–41, even though moving through that single version of the event carefully and prayerfully.

Following the more thorough, studious approach, we might examine all three accounts. This comparative reading reveals interesting details and insights. Thus, Mark shows Jesus "in the stern, asleep on the cushion" and actually saying to the sea, "Quiet, be still." Neither of these points occurs in the other descriptions.

Using biblical commentaries enriches this preparation for prayer. William Barclay's *The Daily Study Bible Series*, for example, contains an enormous amount of information about the cultural and religious scene at the time of Jesus. Such background makes the incident of the calming come alive and sheds additional light on the Lord's words or actions.

He has, to illustrate, two pages on Matthew 8:23–27 which describe the physical setting of the event, provide comments from observers on how rapidly and violently storms arise there, and explain two Greek words that delineate the storm itself and the kind of waves swamping the boat.

2. We select the phrases "Quiet, be still" and "Why are you so terrified? Why are you lacking in faith?" as the words to repeat over and over before sleep, upon arising and at meditation as a reminder of the entire passage or incident.

3. At the time set aside we find our place and have in our hands a copy of the Bible open to the specific text. After some brief relaxation and centering exercises we make ourselves conscious that the Scripture is God's Word and prepare to listen.

4. After reading through carefully and prayerfully the account of the storm and the calming, we lay aside the book, close our eyes and begin the meditation itself.

With our mental powers we try to make the scene appear before us as vividly as possible. We see the boat and the sea; we feel the spray of the waves hit our face and the rising water in the vessel surround our legs; we hear the roaring wind; we watch Jesus' followers furiously but without success bailing out the ever-rising water; we note the fear and panic in their faces; we see, on the other hand, Christ serenely asleep on a cushion; we observe the disciples finally rouse him with the puzzled, worried, almost angry "Teacher, does it not matter to you that we are going to drown?"

We watch the Lord awake, stand up, then powerfully and instantly rebuke the wind and command the sea, "Quiet, be still!" With the disciples we note in amazement and relief how the wind subsides, a great calm develops over the lake and a deep, peaceful stillness descends upon all.

We hear Jesus, after this awesome display of might, chide his stunned followers with these words: "Why are you so terrified? Why are you lacking in faith?"

Like the disciples, we ask in confused admiration, "Who can this be that the wind and sea obey him?"

It may happen that while we are trying to recreate the incident, sentiments of love, adoration, faith, gratitude, etc. may spring up in our hearts. We let them freely surface, bringing forth inner aspirations like "I love you, Lord"; "I believe in you, Jesus"; "Lord Jesus, save me"; "Lord, I adore you." As long as they continue, we need not move on.

Sometimes the scene so enraptures us that we feel a desire simply to gaze upon it without words of any kind, a kind of resting before the Lord. We should not hesitate to remain in that state, aware that this is a very high form of prayer we normally call active contemplation.

On other occasions we may be disposed to remain quite still, sensing that the Lord is speaking mysteriously within us and calling us to listen. This form of prayer, generally termed passive contemplation, can provide a great sense of peace and is a very appropriate way to pray.

Even when our heart seems to be pouring out devout sayings or we are mesmerized by the scene or we feel the Lord is communicating inwardly to us, our mind may wander off to foreign areas and bring in distracting images. When that occurs we should, without strain or irritation, bring back the sea scene before us. This will automatically dispel, at least for a time, those interrupting pictures or thoughts.

If we immediately, after creating the live image of that incident, are able to launch out into those loving aspirations, active contemplation or passive listening, we need not take any other steps.

However, if neither of these occurs, or if after a period they appear to lose some of their holding force, we can begin to ponder the event in a very personal way: How does this incident apply to me? What are the inner storms of my life which need to be stilled or calmed? Those personal feelings of insecurity which make me fearful and unsure? The push of my passions which seem like a turbulent sea within me? The worries about my future—the dread of death, the concern about cancer, the fret over jobs and finances? The resentment which lingers from past hurts?

As we identify those turbulent movements within, we also recognize that the Jesus who calmed the wind and stilled the sea can and does wish here and now through these words to calm and still those violent, upsetting waves within me.

That reasoning application of the incident to our own lives may stimulate or reawaken aspirations, active contemplation or passive listening. We again freely allow those to emerge since they represent the goal of prayer. We also use the same technique mentioned above to dispel distractions as they occur.

5. As our prayer time comes to a close, we draw from the meditation perhaps a practical conclusion for the day's living and a biblical word or phrase to be with us throughout the ensuing hours of work and play.

Often that may be the same one—"Quiet, be still!" and "Why are you so terrified? Why are you lacking in faith?"—which we had selected the night before. A new phrase, however, could suggest itself as a result of the meditation. Whenever possible during the day we bring the short passage to our mind as a way of recalling our period of prayer and the resolution we made.

6. We may not be able to participate in a daily Eucharist as Father Nouwen describes and find there the culmination of our meditation. Nevertheless, at the end of the day, before retiring and before starting over with a new scriptural text for the next day's prayer period, we might have our own informal thanksgiving review session.

We at that time give gratitude to the Lord for our earlier meditation, reflect on how well or poorly we applied this to our life and express thanks or regret accordingly.

Helpful Resources

Messengers of God's Word. Joseph M. Champlin. Paulist Press, 545 Island Road, Ramsey, N.J. 07446. A handbook for lectors which contains a section on prayer and a series of ten reflections each with Scripture and patron saint suitable as resources for the meditative prayer period. A similar handbook for eucharistic ministers, *An Important Office of Immense Love,* by the same publisher, likewise includes a series of fifteen other such reflections with Scripture and patron saint.

A Month with Christ. J. Murray Elwood. Ave Maria Press, Notre Dame, Indiana 46556. An explanation of the Christ in my eyes, heart and hands meditation technique with thirty illustrations.

Saint of the Day. Leonard Foley, O.F.M. St. Anthony Messenger Press, 1615 Republic St., Cincinnati, Ohio 45210. A brief life and lesson for each of the 173 saints in the revised Roman Calendar.

Clowning in Rome. Henri J.M. Nouwen. Doubleday Image Books, Garden City, New York. A plea for daily periods of prayer and a description of his meditation method.

◇ *Method #5:*

Charismatic and Healing Prayer

In 1976–77, while serving as pastor-in-residence at the North American College in Rome, Italy, I occasionally on Sunday afternoons walked into the center of the city and on to the auditorium of the Jesuit staffed Gregorian University. There I prayed together with 200–300 members of a Catholic charismatic prayer group. The session began precisely at 4:00 p.m. and this weekly period of common prayer concluded just as promptly at 5:30 P.M.

The participants were a mix of priests, religious women and men and lay persons, all English speaking, but from every part of the world, most of whom were students at various Roman institutions of higher learning.

During that hour and a half these charismatic people prayed silently and aloud, read or listened to Scripture passages, heard testimonies of God's remarkable action in certain individual lives, received reverently and attentively prophetic utterances from a few persons' lips, sang many hymns to the accompaniment of guitars, stood in prayer, often lifted high hands and arms, sometimes enthusiastically clapped for several moments, spoke or sang in tongues using foreign words unfamiliar to the speaker or to those nearby, and generally looked peaceful and joyous. Afterward priests were available for the sacrament of penance, and those with any kind of hurt or concern could be prayed over by a team of members given over especially to that ministry.

Two years later, back in the same city en route to Africa, I visited with an Irish missionary working in Latin America. He described the rapid growth and marvelous effect of charismatic prayer groups both in Ireland and in mission country churches. A few weeks after that exchange, I spent an evening in Port Elizabeth, South Africa with a small cluster of Catholics who gather each Friday night for this type of prayer.

Those few examples indicate the swift, enormous and worldwide spread of the charismatic movement or renewal.

This charismatic renewal began around 1900 with the Aszuza Street Revival and the era of classic Pentecostal Churches. It entered the mainline Protestant Churches, including the Episcopalian and Lutheran traditions, during the 1950's.

The movement's spread to the Roman Catholic Church had an association with or its roots dating back to Pope Leo XIII's encyclical on the Holy Spirit, the intonation of the *Veni Creator Spiritus* on New Year's Eve, 1899–1900, and Pope John XXIII's prayer for a new Pentecost when he convoked the Second Vatican Council.

Roman Catholic involvement in this charismatic renewal, however, developed in the 1960's and, in the United States, it is generally considered to have begun at Pittsburgh in the spring of 1966.

There at Duquesne University two faculty laymen—actively engaged in various liturgical, spiritual and apostolic endeavors— were disappointed that they did not seem to possess the ability to proclaim the Gospel with power as the early Christians had done. Both then agreed to pray for each other that they might be filled with the Holy Spirit's gifts. To this end the men decided to recite daily the familiar "Come, Holy Spirit" hymn from the Mass of Pentecost.

These men persevered with those promises, and some months later, in February 1967, about twenty people—faculty and student members at Duquesne—experienced a profound religious transformation in their lives. They sensed a real, personal contact with the living Christ. Moreover, charismatic gifts like those known in the early Church appeared; many received the gift of tongues and several received other gifts also, such as prophecy, discernment of spirits and the various gifts of healing.

A small prayer group formed as a result of this. Within a month what had happened in Pittsburgh spread to the University of Notre Dame and to the Catholic student parish at Michigan State University. From these three centers, the renewal quickly leaped to Cleveland, Ohio, the University of Iowa and the University of Portland, Oregon. Simultaneously, however, similar experiences occurred in many places throughout the United States and abroad.[1]

The near miraculous growth of the charismatic renewal, clearly not the result of human planning or programming and surely one of those Spirit-inspired developments like the resurgence of interest in Mary described earlier, stands out through these statistics which follow.

The first national conference held in 1967 attracted about 100 people.[2] The convention at Notre Dame in 1970 drew 1,279 participants.[3] In 1973, an international conference, also at Notre Dame, brought 22,000 from 35 countries with 600 priests and 10 bishops. The next year, 1974, that number at Notre Dame rose to 30,000 with a comparable increase in priests and bishops.[4]

My Roman and subsequent African experiences several years later confirmed in a personal way this spread of the spiritual renewal both in actual numbers and in its worldwide dimension.

Common Elements of Charismatic Prayer

There are no definite rules according to which one can be classified as a charismatic or by which we judge our conversation with God to be charismatic prayer. Every prayer group has its own style, and each member of any prayer group likewise possesses her or his own unique manner of praying.

Nevertheless, in 1982 at the National Charismatic Conference advisory leaders did cite five basic points as criteria needed for a prayer unit to term itself a Catholic charismatic prayer group: Individual and personal conversion to Jesus Christ as one's Lord and Savior; receiving a personal outpouring of (being baptized in) the Holy Spirit; reception and use of the spiritual and charismatic gifts; development of a solid personal spiritual life; adherence to Catholic faith and practice.

Here is a listing and description of some general or more common elements we normally associate with or detect in charismatic prayer groups and individuals:

◇ **An active belief in the Holy Spirit's working presence among us today.**

Charismatics read often the Acts of the Apostles and obviously find there frequent references to the Holy Spirit operating in the early Church.

It begins most noticeably, of course, on Pentecost (Acts 2:1–13) with the strong, driving wind and tongues of fire. "All were filled with the Holy Spirit. They began to express themselves in foreign tongues and made bold proclamation as the Spirit prompted them."

However, throughout Acts one also notes regularly explicit mention of the Holy Spirit. For example:

Stephen, "filled with the Holy Spirit," looked to the sky above . . . (Acts 7:55).

Philip, after baptizing the eunuch, found that "the Spirit of the Lord" snatched him away (Acts 8:39).

Ananias told Saul after his conversion, "I have been sent by the Lord Jesus, who appeared to you on the way here, to help you recover your sight and be filled with the Holy Spirit" (Acts 9:17).

Peter, in describing his experience with the Gentile Cornelius, remarked, "The Spirit instructed me to accompany them . . . " (Acts 11:12).

Saul (also known as Paul) and Barnabas, "sent forth by the Holy Spirit," went down to the port . . . (Acts 13:4).

The disciples, despite opposition and persecution, "could not but be filled with joy and the Holy Spirit" (Acts 13:52).

One could go on almost endlessly with other citations from Acts mentioning expressly the Holy Spirit. It would be profitable for my readers to use prayer and Bible time to study both the Gospel of Luke and Acts to catch these frequent references to the Holy Spirit.

Charismatics, however, also concentrate on St. Paul's teaching to the Corinthians about the variety of spiritual gifts given to followers of Christ for building up the kingdom.

> Now, brothers, I do not want to leave you in ignorance about
> spiritual gifts. You know that when you were pagans you were

led astray to mute idols, as impulse drove you. That is why I tell you that nobody who speaks in the Spirit of God ever says, "Cursed be Jesus." And no one can say: "Jesus is Lord," except in the Holy Spirit.

There are different gifts but the same Spirit; there are different ministries but the same Lord; there are different works but the same God who accomplishes all of them in everyone. To each person the manifestation of the Spirit is given for the common good. To one the Spirit gives wisdom in discourse, to another the power to express knowledge. Through the Spirit one receives faith; by the same Spirit another is given the gift of healing and still another miraculous powers. Prophecy is given to one, to another power to distinguish one spirit from another. One receives the gift of tongues, another that of interpreting the tongues. But it is one and the same Spirit who produces all these gifts, distributing them to each as he wills.

The body is one and has many members, but all the members, many though they are, are one body; and so it is with Christ. It was in one Spirit that all of us, whether Jew or Greek, slave or free, were baptized into one body. All of us have been given to drink of the one Spirit (1 Corinthians 12:1–13).

Those in the charismatic renewal believe that the Holy Spirit is working among us in much the same way that the Spirit operated during the early years of the Church. They rely as individuals and as groups upon the Spirit for personal guidance and courage.

◇ A personal relationship with the Lord Jesus.

This flows almost automatically out of that quote from 1 Corinthians about being able to say "Jesus is Lord" only in the Holy Spirit.

Jesus, for the charismatic, is not merely the Son of God and founder of the Church. Christ becomes more—a brother and friend, intimately interested in the smallest details of our life. We develop a close and highly personal relationship with God through Jesus.

Leon Joseph Cardinal Suenens, former archbishop of Brussels-Malines, Belgium and one of the outstanding Vatican II leaders of the Church, experienced that development in his spiritual life and found that it led him easily to prayer of praise and thanksgiving.

> This thanksgiving easily takes the form of a litany in which I enumerate a name, a memory, a date, a coincidence. I say to God "thank you" for advice given in a moment of crisis, a book read casually which had a message for me, a telephone call, a letter, a suffering, an encouragement. And permeating and binding all these is my thanks to him for a joy and a peace that no one can take from me because they are beyond the reach of man.
>
> This is like saying the rosary: the beads slipping through my fingers, one mystery succeeding another: joyful, sorrowful and glorious. Each bead recalls some attention shown me by God, a sign, a meeting. I end with a "Glory be to the Father," a thanksgiving for the love of God which has been waiting for me at every turn of my life, at every detour on the road.[5]

◇ **A great love for Scripture.**

Charismatics believe in the divine inspiration of the Bible and turn to God's written Word frequently for wisdom and strength.

Visitors to prayer meetings will find that most participants bring their own large and well used Bibles. These usually have tabs for easier location of specific books, pages of print in the text underlined, and many marginal notes.

I know of one charismatic married woman, the mother of three, who rises early each day and reads Scripture with commentaries for about an hour. She is not an isolated illustration.

◇ **An ease with and desire for spontaneous, enthusiastic, community, externalized prayer.**

At the beginning of this chapter I described the pattern of worship at the prayer group in Rome's Gregorian University. Such praying out loud, singing, clapping of hands, stretching out arms toward the sky and communicating in tongues is standard procedure for charismatic gatherings around the world.

Cardinal Suenens describes and gives a supportive explanation for this type of prayer:

> The spontaneity of this prayer, expressed by rhythmic movement, clapping of hands, hands raised or joined together in a sign of unity, is especially appreciated by young people. It helps those who lend themselves to it to step out of their individualism, their inhibitions and their excessive cerebralism.
>
> Sometimes people object to this as being too emotional. It is worthwhile analyzing this objection more closely. For if someone objects to the emotional character of a particular style of prayer, it can well be that he feels himself threatened by its personal quality. We are so accustomed to formalism, ritualism, and conventionalism that deeply personal prayer can present a challenge to our inhibitions. We are afraid to be ourselves before God and before one another and hence we resort to a defense mechanism which labels as "emotionalism" what in reality is an authentic personal quality of prayer. We tend to avoid emotion in our relations with God, or at least we prefer to depersonalize prayer, just as we have today stripped and laid bare so many of our churches.[6]

◇ **A love for singing.**

Charismatic prayer meetings and Masses are not short. Participants sing often, loud and long, frequently with simple, almost mantra-like hymns ("Alleluia" and "Jesus is Lord" would be more common examples). The renewal has thus contributed significantly to the fostering of congregational song in our parishes and among Catholics.

◇ **Praying in tongues.**

In many ways, this phenomenon has become the most distinguishing characteristic of charismatic prayer because of its unusual nature. Those who practice or encourage speaking or singing in tongues during prayer obviously point to the Pentecost experience and Paul's teaching for support.

Some distinguish three types of speaking or singing in tongues.

In the first, as happened at Pentecost, a person speaks in one language and is simultaneously understood by many. They listen and grasp the meaning but are unfamiliar with the words spoken.

In the second, an individual praises God in a language neither she nor he nor anyone present understands. This reflects St. Paul's instruction in Romans 8:26. "The Spirit too helps us in our weakness, for we do not know how to pray as we ought; but the Spirit himself makes intercession for us with groanings which cannot be expressed in speech. He who searches hearts knows what the Spirit means, for the Spirit intercedes for the saints as God himself wills."

In the third, an individual sings or speaks in tongues and some person present understands and interprets for others the content of the message.

When we refer to praying in tongues, it is usually the second type under consideration.

People who pray in tongues are not miracle workers, are not pathological and are not out of control.

It is a relatively ordinary phenomenon today.

It occurs within people who are psychologically sound and emotionally stable.

It remains always under a person's control. We can turn the gift of tongues on or off like a water faucet and use it at our discretion, often mixing this type of praying with other forms of prayer.

Cardinal Suenens describes his own experience with prayer in tongues and offers a defense or a plea for its acceptance:

> We should attempt some evaluation of its spiritual value. There are numerous testimonies—and I would join my own to them— which witness to the fact that this mode of prayer brings a freedom from spiritually inhibiting bonds, which blocks our relationship with God and with our fellowmen and makes us find a whole new sense of liberation.
>
> If, at the outset, a person accepts this act of humility—the risk of appearing foolish or childish—he soon discovers the joy of praying in a way that transcends words and human reasoning, bringing great peace and an openness to spiritual communication with others.

Nor are other forms of prayer excluded. Moreover, it can be practiced alone or in a group. When, in a prayer meeting, it takes the form of an improvised chant in tongues, it can assume, in musical terms, a rare beauty as well as a religious depth by which no one who listens without prejudice can fail to be impressed.

If St. Paul treats this gift as the least of all—though he used it himself—might this not be because it is, in a sense, a way that leads to the other gifts, a small doorway as it were, which can only be entered by stooping: like the door into the Church of the Nativity at Bethlehem? Humility and a childlike spirit characterize the Kingdom of God: "If you do not become as little children . . . ." We know this saying of Jesus, and it has considerable relevance here. The gift of tongues, which has nothing to do with the intellect, makes a breach in the "reserve" we assume as a system of defense. It helps us cross a threshold and, in doing so, to attain a new freedom in our surrender to God. This surrender hands over body and soul to the action of the Holy Spirit. It is only a first step by which we learn how to yield to the other gifts, but nonetheless it is precious because it gives expression, in its own way, to the inner freedom of the children of God.[7]

◇ **Resting in the Spirit.**

Frequently termed "Slain in the Spirit"—a somewhat alarming or disconcerting phrase for many uninitiated—this phenomenon usually occurs in the context of healing prayer.

A respected charismatic leader describes the happening in this way: "The person experiences God's presence and love as direct touches on his or her internal senses. This causes the individual to be unable to remain standing, thus resulting in his or her falling back or being unable to move if already sitting or kneeling. The person is intensely aware of the Lord and is also aware of what is going on around him or her. It is *not* an unconscious, semiconscious, trance-like or sleep-like state. Where authentic, it is an experience that involves spiritual content and frequently spiritual, inner or physical healing. Like other spiritual experiences, it must be tested for its authenticity and discerned as to its effect."

◇ **Prophecy**.

St. Paul speaks of prophecy as a gift of the Holy Spirit, and makes this observation: "The prophet, on the other hand, speaks to men for their upbuilding, their encouragement, their consolation. He who speaks in a tongue builds up himself, but he who prophesies builds up the Church" (1 Corinthians 14:3–4).

At charismatic prayer assemblies, generally several persons will indicate they have received a word from the Lord and wish to share that message with the group. The communication ordinarily does not have a future or prediction element to it; instead, the prophecy, reflecting St. Paul's New Testament teaching, also bears a certain resemblance to Old Testament prophets and most of their messages. The prophet, deemed in those days of the Hebrew Scriptures a "mouth-piece of God," simply conveyed the word given which often was a message of hope or correction, frequently a warning to repent or a promise of support and sometimes, but not usually, a prediction. The many prophecies I have heard in the past half dozen years fall into that category. The listeners normally respond by applauding, nodding heads, or uttering an "Alleluia," "Amen" or "Yes" to the prophecy uttered.

Approval of the Church

I have been asked from time to time about the status of the charismatic renewal in the Catholic Church. "Does the Church give approval to this type of prayer and these types of people?"

The answer cannot be very specific, because the inquiries are too vague.

Every charismatic group differs and each member, as well, varies in her or his approach to prayer. Thus we could make a negative judgment about the orthodoxy of a certain prayer group, for example, but that would not necessarily apply to all the participants. Conversely, a member whose views and practices are questionable does not automatically mean that the entire prayer group is moving in the wrong direction.

Having given this observation, let me say that the charismatic prayer renewal does enjoy sound official Church support, but that it likewise possesses certain tendencies which may lead members astray.

In November 1969, about two years after those initial meetings at Duquesne, Notre Dame and elsewhere, the American Bishops' Committee on Doctrine submitted a report to the full body of bishops on "the so-called Pentecostal movement among our Catholic faithful."

Here are a few excerpts from that document:

> Many would prefer to speak of it as a charismatic renewal . . .
>
> It must be admitted that theologically the movement has legitimate reasons for existence. It has a strong biblical basis. It would be difficult to inhibit the work of the Spirit which manifested itself so abundantly in the early Church. The participants in the Catholic pentecostal movement claim that they receive certain charismatic gifts. Admittedly, there have been abuses, but the cure is not a denial of their existence but their proper use. We still need further research on the matter of charismatic gifts. Certainly, the recent Vatican Council presumes that the Spirit is active continuously in the Church.
>
> Perhaps our most prudent way to judge the validity of the claims of the pentecostal movement is to observe the effects on those who participate in the prayer meetings. There are many indications that this participation leads to a better understanding of the role the Christian plays in the Church. Many have experienced progress in their spiritual life. They are attracted to the reading of the Scriptures and a deeper understanding of their faith. They seem to grow in their attachment to certain established devotional patterns such as devotion to the real presence and the rosary.
>
> It is the conclusion of the Committee on Doctrine that the movement should at this point not be inhibited but allowed to develop.[8]

In 1973, Pope Paul VI addressed representatives of the charismatic renewal assembled for an international meeting at Grottoferrata, Italy. Here, also, are a few excerpts from that speech:

> We rejoice with you, dear friends, at the renewal of spiritual life manifested in the Church today, in different forms and in

various environments. Certain common notes appear in this renewal: the taste for deep prayer, personal and in groups, a return to contemplation and an emphasizing of praise of God, the desire to devote oneself completely to Christ, a great availability for the calls of the Holy Spirit, more assiduous reading of the Scripture, generous brotherly devotion, the will to make a contribution to the service of the Church. In all that, we can recognize the mysterious and discreet work of the Spirit, who is the soul of the Church.

Even in the best experiences of renewal, moreover, weeds may be found among the good seed. So a work of discernment is indispensable; it devolves upon those who are in charge of the Church, "to whose special competence it belongs, not indeed to extinguish the Spirit, but to test all things and hold fast to that which is good" (cf. 1 Thes 5:12 and 19–21) (*Lumen Gentium*, 12). In this way the common good of the Church, to which the gifts of the Spirit are ordained (cf. 1 Cor 12:7), makes progress.[9]

During the rest of the 1970's and now early 1980's individual bishops have followed that path of simultaneous encouragement and discernment stressed by the doctrinal committee and the Holy Father. They have done so through supporting charismatic groups in various ways and at the same time seeking to evaluate in an on-going manner the spiritual soundness of different elements in the renewal.

Some of the harmful or unhealthy tendencies that can emerge among charismatic prayer groups and in individual members are an excessive emotionalism, a rejection of the Church's authority and teaching in certain areas, a subtle pride which considers inner messages as direct communications from God without the need to test them against other indications of the Lord's will, a minimizing or denial of the traditional place that Mary and the saints have held in the Church, an elitism by which they unconsciously regard themselves as superior to non-charismatics, an exaggerated emphasis on the charismatic gifts such as tongues and prophecy, a too individualistic and narrow interpretation of the Bible, a denial or discounting of the value of the sacraments, and a false ecumenism which ignores real doctrinal differences between Churches.

This double duty incumbent upon Catholic Church leaders of encouraging all that is good among charismatics and yet keeping a cautious eye on those potentially false or hurtful trends requires the wisdom of Solomon.

Healing Prayer

About four years ago wife and mother Jan Porter learned that a throat cancer, previously treated and ostensibly cured, had, according to a routine x-ray review, apparently reappeared. This spelled potential disaster for the middle aged woman and created deep anxieties in her husband, large family and many friends.

On the day of surgery, a half-dozen friends gathered in their parish church after the early morning Mass and prayed at length specifically for the riddance of that cancer and Jan's return to full health.

When the surgeon opened up this woman and examined her esophagus area, he found no trace of the ominous growth. Doctors who thoroughly studied the tests were absolutely convinced that a new cancer had developed; they just as absolutely could give no explanation for its disappearance.

Jan's family and friends believe they know the reason for this wonderful development. They judge that it was due to the power of their faith and prayer.

Only God can provide the true explanation of this real or apparent healing, and for that revelation we must wait until the Kingdom comes.

However, Mrs. Porter's friends have solid biblical support for their belief that God will heal the hurting through prayer. The scriptural argumentation runs in this fashion:

1. Jesus had the power to heal and did in fact cure the sick. People "came to hear him and be healed of their diseases. Those who were troubled with unclean spirits were cured; indeed, the whole crowd was trying to touch him because power went out from him which cured all" (Luke 6:18–19).

2. Christ shared this power with the twelve apostles. He

"gave them authority to expel unclean spirits and to cure sickness and disease of every kind . . . cure the sick, raise the dead, heal the leprous, expel demons" (Matthew 10:1–8).

3. The Lord, because of the vast and ever-expanding needs, extended that healing power to the seventy-two, a symbolic as well as real number of disciples. "After this, the Lord appointed a further seventy-two and sent them in pairs before him to every town and place he intended to visit . . . . 'Into whatever city you go, after they welcome you, eat what they set before you, and cure the sick there' " (Luke 10:1–8).

4. Jesus promised that followers of him in the centuries to come would cure the sick through faith, prayer and the laying on of hands: "Signs like these will accompany those who have professed their faith; they will use my name to expel demons . . . and the sick upon whom they lay their hands will recover" (Mark 16:17–18).

During my early years in the priesthood I believed in miraculous cures, but judged them to be rather exceptional cases which normally occurred at holy places like Lourdes in France or St. Anne's in Canada and were connected with some saintly person. Claims of cures by ordinary people made me suspicious, and I tended to attribute the supposed healing to certain unknown natural causes.

In the past decade, personal experiences like that incident with Jan Porter, study of those biblical texts above, the testimonies of others and the writings of people like Dennis and Matthew Linn, Francis MacNutt and Barbara Shlemon have brought about a shift in my thinking.[10]

I believe now that God in a special way wishes today to heal people's hurts through the prayer of the faithful. I also believe that there is always a healing whenever we pray for it as individuals or as a group, although that cure may be inner only and not a physical restoration to health. I likewise believe that the sense of touch or laying on of hands possesses a somehow unique power for healing people's interior and exterior burdens. I believe that often the greatest response to our prayer for healing is a recognition of sickness or hurt as a mystery in God's plan of love for us to experience rather than a problem requiring solution. I believe, finally, that our prayer provides courage to bear bravely the sickness or trouble pressing upon us.

Francis MacNutt has written an extremely readable paperback *The Prayer That Heals: Praying for Healing in the Family* which could be very useful for someone who wishes to understand the why and the how of this prayer for healing. The excerpt below, taken from his chapter on "Touch," gives a sample of MacNutt's style and approach:

> So, if you have never prayed with someone and put your hand upon them while you prayed, I encourage you to try it. If your child is sick, laying your hand upon the child is such a natural thing to do anyway. It should be just as natural to pray for a husband, wife or friend—once you get over that initial shyness. Holding a person's hand or putting your arm around a shoulder is such a natural gesture. If the person is sick and it can be done decently, put your hand near the affected area while you are praying.
>
> If you do start praying with people, you should soon see enough healings take place through your touch to encourage you and strengthen your faith even more.
>
> For instance, you may pray with a person who has a tumor and, as you put your hand upon that tumor, you may gradually see it disappear. At first, you won't be sure: Is it just your imagination? But then, as you pray, you find, to your amazement, that it really is shrinking. Usually, it just takes one or two experiences like that to convince you that God still wants ordinary people like you—simple believers—to lay hands upon the sick who will then recover.
>
> There is one beautiful discovery about healing touch that I would especially like to share, and that is how wonderful it is for a husband (or friends) to pray for a pregnant wife and her unborn baby. Sometimes the baby gives its first kick as the mother is prayed for—life responding to life. Of course, if the mother is alone she can put her hand upon her stomach and pray for the child. A friend, Dr. Conrad Baars, says that a mother can actually play with her unborn child by placing her hand, first on one side for a while, then on the other. The baby will turn in the womb, gradually shifting around until its back

is toward the mother's loving hand. Parents who have prayed for their children before birth report that these children seem to be happier, cry less and have better dispositions than their children born in previous years without such prayer.[11]

A practical application of this healing prayer of touch is the custom of family members signing the cross on the forehead of one another at especially significant moments during the day. As you may recall from this book's introduction, the mother from Bainbridge reported how after our Lenten workshop she returned home and started to trace the sign of the cross on her five year old daughter's forehead daily as she departed for school. The little girl reciprocated.

In my travels I have learned of another couple who have done this regularly with their children for years. Now their sons and daughters are in colleges, but when home for vacation these young men and women always ask for the parents' cross blessing, especially before examinations.

The imposition or laying on of hands, the use of the sacramentals of holy water and blessed oil—all connected with prayer for healing—have been given restored understanding and appreciation as a direct, positive result of the charismatic renewal. The vocation of all Christians to pray one for another and to minister God's mercy or loving kindness to those who are hurting is truly a gift of rediscovery from the Holy Spirit in our day.

Helpful Resources

The Prayer That Heals: Prayer for Healing in the Family. Francis MacNutt. Ave Maria Press, Notre Dame, Indiana 46556 ($2.95). A short, easy to read, inexpensive paperback which offers an understandable explanation of healing prayer and practical ways for individuals or families to introduce this practice.

A New Pentecost? Leon Joseph Cardinal Suenens. The Seabury Press, 815 Second Avenue, New York, N.Y. 10017 ($8.95). A sound, sympathetic and supportive explanation of the charismatic movement and charismatic prayer.

Finding New Life in the Spirit: A Guidebook for the Life in the Spirit Seminars. Charismatic Renewal Services, 237 N. Michigan St., South Bend, Indiana 46601 ($.75). The best way to make a judgment about charismatic prayer is to participate in several prayer meetings (not just one) and even to make a "Life in the Spirit" seminar, a seven week process of prayer, Bible reading, instruction and testimonies. This small pamphlet, of which there are over 1,000,000 in print, is the text generally used and the procedure followed.

◊ *Method #6:*

Centering Prayer

The *Time* magazine article cited earlier on the value of meditation for coping with stress described a simple reflective technique for producing what is termed a "relaxation response." It consists of four steps:

"Assume a comfortable position."

"Close your eyes."

"Concentrate on a single word, sound or phrase."

"Cast off all other thoughts."

Cardiologist Herbert Benson encourages his patients who practice that particular type of meditative method to select a word, sound or image that appeals to them personally. "One of his Jewish patients focuses on the word *shalom*; a Greek chants *Kyrie eleison* ('Lord, have mercy on us'); a Catholic recites the prayer 'Lord Jesus, have mercy'; others involve the response by listening to soothing tapes of ocean waves."[1]

Readers will recognize here a few of the recommendations for praying described in Part I of this book. Those who already have an experience of centering prayer should likewise detect in it the fundamental framework of that method which I now plan to treat in some detail.

We mentioned in a previous section that meditation seeks to employ actively our inner powers—imagination, memory, reason and will. We gave there both general principles and actual illustrations on how to create vivid mental pictures during prayer, how to ponder the scene in a prayerful way and how to converse with the Lord in a loving manner.

Centering prayer resembles meditation in a certain fashion. It engages our inner powers and results in a silent, withdrawn and reflective type of praying.

However, centering prayer differs from meditation in that it avoids mental pictures, interior reasoning and, for the most part, affective conversations with God. How this form of prayer—rapidly increasing in popularity—actually does so should become evident through the explanation which follows.

Trappist monk M. Basil Pennington, from St. Joseph's Abbey in Spencer, Massachusetts, a widely traveled teacher and lecturer as well as prolific author, would probably be considered the foremost proponent today of centering prayer in the United States. While several of his writings touch on that subject, *Centering Prayer: Reviewing an Ancient Christian Prayer Form*, clearly explains the concept and could serve as a sort of manual for beginners. I am relying almost exclusively on his presentation in that book for the material below. [2]

Pennington summarizes the essential notion of centering prayer in these words:

> In Centering Prayer we go beyond thought and image, beyond the senses and the rational mind, to that center of our being where God is working a wonderful work. There God our Father is not only bringing us forth at each moment in his wonderful creative love, but by virtue of the grace of filiation, which we received at baptism, he is indeed making us sons and daughters, one with his own Son, pouring out in our hearts the Spirit of his Son, so that we can in the fullest sense cry, "Abba, Father." He says to us, in fact more than in word: "You are my son; this day have I begotten you." At this level of our being, where we are our truest selves, we are essentially prayer, total response to the Father in our oneness with the Son, in that love who is the Holy Spirit. [3]

All that we encouraged earlier in this book concerning time, place and preparation for prayer in general applies very specifically to centering prayer.

With regard to *time*, for example, the Trappist leader proposes two twenty-minute meditations each day, normally in the morning and evening, and then expands upon his proposal:

> We have encouraged twenty-minute meditations. Most find this a good pace. Some find themselves settling for a little less

or a little more. Religious and others who recognize prayer as a major part of their particular vocation and service usually opt for longer periods. But shorter periods are not to be ruled out. Ten minutes is better than five, and five better than none, though we might want to reexamine our priorities if that seems to be all we are able to allow ourselves for something that so touches the center of our being and life. Along with our two basic meditations, we may well find our rhythm opening out into a third, perhaps shorter one, at midday, or even many quite short ones as we move along through the day from one area of activity to another or from one engagement to another. The prayer word itself may at times come on its own to summon us to what my brother calls a "quickie." As the author of *The Cloud* reminds us, time "needs only a brief fraction of a moment" to move into eternity.[4]

Any *place* is appropriate for centering prayer, but the author does recommend a good chair which makes it possible to sit with the back essentially straight during the meditation session.[5]

Finally, Father Pennington suggests the kind of relaxation techniques and closing of the eyes we outlined in Part I as the immediate *preparatory steps* prior to the period of centering prayer.

The actual centering prayer method consists of these components:

Step 1: *"At the beginning of the prayer we take a minute or two to quiet down and then move in faith to God dwelling in our depths."*[6]

During that moment or two we explicitly speak to God, offer this period of prayer and express our faith in the Lord's presence dwelling within us. "In a fraction of a minute—and ordinarily we should not take much more than that—we pass into a prayer of quiet recollection, of presence. And it is there we wish to stay, in a state of loving attention."[7]

I have personally found his caution about this being only a "fraction of a minute" very important to keep in mind. Frequently I catch myself in the drowsy early morning period or the distracted later afternoon hours having spent perhaps five minutes in that explicit expression of faith and love before moving on to the more precise centering.

Pennington offers in an appendix a few helpful illustrations of this expressed movement of faith and love at centering prayer's beginning:

> We offer here a few examples of the way the movement of faith and love at the beginning of the Centering Prayer might be expressed. These are only examples of individual expressions. No one should try to use them or imitate them precisely. Each should allow the movement of faith and love to well up from his or her own heart and use those words that spontaneously come to express such a movement.
>
> 1. Lord, I believe that you are truly present in me, at the center of my being, bringing me forth in your love. For these few minutes, I want to be completely to you. Draw me, Lord, into your presence. Let me experience your presence and love.
>
> 2. Father, I thank you for your wonderful presence. I want to be completely to you in adoration, praise, love, thanksgiving. Let me experience your presence, your love, your care. I come to you, Father, in Christ Jesus, my Lord.
>
> 3. Jesus, you are truly present at the center of my being, at the ground of my being. I love you, Lord. I am one with you in your love. Jesus, be my all. Jesus, draw me to yourself. Jesus. Jesus.[8]

Step 2: *"After resting for a bit in the center in faith-full love, we take up a single, simple word that expresses this response and begin to let it repeat itself within."*[9]

The Trappist describes the kind of word desired, the concept of "center" and the goal we seek to reach:

> Although Centering Prayer is an extremely simple and pure method of prayer, it is not yet wholly free from some use of symbols, at least not until it opens out into the transcendent experience. This may take place almost immediately, but still in the first moments, as we move into the Prayer, we use some thought, affection, and image. During the progress of the Prayer, we seek to employ—only to the extent truly neces-

sary—the subtlest and most human of symbols, a very simple
word. As the author of *The Cloud* says: "A one-syllable word
such as 'God' or 'love' is best." But in moving into the Prayer,
most find the rather subtle imaginative symbol of the "center"
very effective. This place—which we make no attempt at pin-
pointing physically or imaginatively—is deep within, deep
within our spirit. It is the place of encounter with the living
Triune God. It is the place where at every moment we come
forth into being by his loving creative action. It is the "ground
of our being," to use another Merton simile. [10]

We can see here how centering prayer significantly differs
from the reasoning, discursive meditation of our earlier chapter.

Some authors suggest that we pray in a conscious and direct
way to the Holy Spirit and ask for guidance in selecting the word
best for us—"God, Jesus, Lord, love, etc." That word should be a
single, simple word rather than a phrase. However, as in all
prayer we must avoid an excessive concern about the precise
word, the correct posture and the proper technique. Those are
merely helpful, human tools to assist us in praying and not indispensable ingredients.

Distractions in prayer are a problem for every human being.
The next step deals with that issue in centering prayer.

Step 3. *"Whenever in the course of the Prayer we become
aware of something else, we simply and gently return to the Presence by the use of the prayer word."* [11]

The following is a lengthy quotation. However, in it Pennington not only explains how to use the prayer word when distractions develop, but also unfolds the intimate essence of centering
prayer.

In Centering Prayer we sink down into the quiet depths, where
there is only a simple, peaceful flow from our Source into the
Ocean of Infinite Love. What serenity, what tranquillity, what
peace; what vitality, what power, what refreshment! But, on
the surface, a lot of activity is still going on. Thoughts are still
careening along, feelings are being evoked, sounds are hitting

our eardrums. And every once in a while, a flashy vessel or a particularly interesting one arrests our attention and we find ourselves surfacing—or perhaps we have fully surfaced and all but climbed aboard the enticing boat before we are aware of having left the peaceful depths.

It is at this point that we use our prayer word. We do not so much turn from the thought or feeling. We do not think (another thought) of letting it go. We simply—with the gentlest repetition of our prayer word, maybe only the faintest recollection of it—return to the Presence. The author of *The Cloud* says, "It is best when this word is wholly interior, without a definite thought or actual sound." We simply, peacefully sink again into the depths. It is as gentle and effortless as that: a sinking down into the depths. If we but let ourselves go, we have a natural propensity to rest quietly in our Source. And so, throughout our prayer time, the thoughts, the feelings, the sounds, the images continue. We just let them flow along. Our attention is elsewhere.

We use the prayer word when we need it and to the extent we need it, and always gently. The thoughts and feelings and images will always be there. But it is only when we become aware of them, when they have drawn our attention away from the depths, from the Beloved, to themselves, that we need to deliberately—but always gently—employ our prayer word to return to the Presence. For the rest, we let the word simply be there. It may repeat itself, faster or slower, stronger or weaker; it may take up the rhythm of our heart or of our breath (though we do not in any way seek to bring this about, or give any attention to either of these), or it may fuzz out and be more of a silent image than an actual sound. No matter! Our attention is to the Presence, known in faith, embraced in love; the word is incidental, a useful means, used when a means is useful.

In prayer we seek God. We do not seek peace, quiet, tranquillity, enlightenment; we do not seek anything for ourselves. We seek to give ourselves, or, rather, we do simply give ourselves, even without attending to ourselves, so whole is our intent upon the one to whom we give: God. He is the all of our prayer. If thoughts and images and feelings career around in our head and in our heart, little matter. We pay no attention to them. We do not seek to get rid of them any more than we seek

to entertain them. As we give ourselves in our loving attention
to God, we also give them to him. And let him do with them
what he wants to do with them.[12]

I have found this procedure extremely valuable at all times,
but especially when I am preoccupied with powerfully distracting
images or am fighting off, rather unsuccessfully, drowsiness and
sleep. When I become aware of a distraction or realize that I
seemed to have momentarily dropped off, I gently recall the word
and resume. As Father Pennington mentions, each return from
distraction or drowsiness is another gesture of faith and love—for
me repeated, I must confess, rather frequently during the centering prayer period.

The fact that we do fall asleep on occasion during a meditation
or centering prayer session need not be a cause of anxiety. If we
have prepared as well as we can and made that explicit offering of
the reflective moments to follow, then the inability to remain
awake or concentrate is merely a sign of our variable weakened
human condition, and our prayer continues nevertheless to be a
fine faith or love offering to the Lord. When, on the other hand, a
pattern of sleep during centering prayer emerges, we need to ana-
lyze our living habits to discern if more rest may be required for
us to function effectively.

Sometimes during centering prayer or meditation, great
ideas, thoughts, projects and inspirations spring up in our consciousness. Despite their nobleness, practical value and seeming
brilliance, it is best to put them aside gently as distractions. If God
wishes those notions to impact our lives, then we can be confident
that the Spirit later, outside centering prayer time, will bring
them back to us.

Step 4: *"At the end of the Centering Prayer we take several
minutes to come out, mentally praying the 'Our Father' or some
other prayer."*[13]

Father Pennington stresses the fact that there should be a
brief, easy but concentrated transition up and out of the deeply reflective state connected with centering prayer. That movement

leads to a few moments of reasoning and affective prayer and on to perhaps a specific overflow into our on-going lives.

> We do not want to jump from deep prayer right back into activity. On one level—the physiological—it could be distressing. When we settle down in deep meditation, our whole system settles down: the breathing quiets, the heart slows down, our body almost seems to sleep. *Ego dormio sed cor meum vigilat*—"I sleep, but my heart watches." We want to rise back, gently, to the active level, bringing back with us some of that deep inner quiet and peace, harmony and rhythm.
>
> More important, we want to bring back to the conceptual and affective level what we can of the deep experience of God we have been enjoying. So it is recommended that at the end of our predetermined time of meditation, we move to interior prayer of an affective and conceptual type. Thus the experience we have had is able to find some expression on these levels of our lives and from them flow in a more reflectively experiential way into our on-going lives.[14]

The Trappist recommends the Our Father as probably the most apt formula for this transition and illustrates how this can be done through a slow, line by line praying of that text.[15] Nevertheless, he concludes, "We can use any prayer, a free-flowing prayer in our own words and images—anything that will bring something of the deep experience quietly up into the plane of activity into which we are to move."[16]

During those Lenten workshops, I discovered that the majority of participants had never heard of centering prayer and thus had obviously not practiced this method at least in a conscious way. After a short explanation, we then tried about a five-minute experience with it.

The reactions were almost universally positive. One college student indicated that centering prayer for her was more satisfying than the earlier discursive meditation we had taught and tried. An older man commented on the deep peace he sensed during and after the brief experiment.

I recall most vividly, however, the observation of a middle

aged housewife and mother who understands now that she has in effect been practicing centering prayer for most of her adult life without realizing it. "In quiet times, I just sit and say silently over and over and over again the name of Jesus."

Helpful Resources

What Is Contemplation? Thomas Merton, Templegate Books, Springfield, Illinois. The late famous Trappist author distinguishes contemplation and meditation, describes how we enter contemplation, shows the difference between contemplation and quietism, and draws upon some of the classic spiritual writers. This 79-page paperback is available at $4.95 from Charismatic Renewal Services, 237 N. Michigan, South Bend, Indiana 46601.

Centering Prayer: Renewing an Ancient Christian Prayer Form. M. Basil Pennington, O.C.S.O. An Image paperback available at $4.50 from Doubleday and Company, Garden City, N.Y. This text obviously has been the main resource for my treatment in the present chapter. The entire book will be helpful for those who wish to begin centering prayer, but the core explanation can be found in Chapter IV, "A New Packaging."

◊ *Method #7:*

Journal Keeping

Participants at worldwide Marriage Encounter weekends learn a communication technique called dialogue. In that process, spouses separate, write down during a specified period of time their feelings in response to a common, personal question, then meet and in a prayerful, caring way share the content of this "love letter" with each other.

Such writing and exchanging often enables partners to surface, clarify and communicate inner emotions and attitudes which otherwise would probably remain buried deeply within the person. This sharing also can create a closeness or oneness that brings true joy to the individual and to the couple.

Leaders encourage the spouses to continue their dialogues afterward on a daily basis.

Most of the people on these weekends obviously are married couples. But often a few priests and celibate deacons as well as religious women and men will be present on a Marriage Encounter weekend. How and with whom do they dialogue?

At the encounter itself, there is a pairing off with each other or a matching up with the priest leader. Some of their questions are identical with those used by the married couples, and others have been modified to meet the specific vocation and life style of a priest, deacon or religious.

After the weekend, the priest, for example, who carries the dialogue technique over into daily life normally will direct his letter to the Lord. The writing or question may be about a spiritual matter of some concern at that occasion or it may be in response to a passage from Sacred Scripture read just beforehand.

I have a close priest friend whose personal and prayer lives have been deeply transformed by the marriage encounter experience. After his original weekend, he underwent training to become a presenting priest for subsequent encounters, exercised a leadership role in the movement and participated as the clergy director in nearly one hundred weekends extending over a period of years.

He had, previous to Marriage Encounter, served conscientiously as a parish priest and in a dutiful manner carried out the standard prayer responsibilities expected by the Church of its clergy. But there was little enthusiasm, minimal reading of Scripture other than in the divine office, and almost no reflective prayer or meditation.

Almost immediately after his initial Marriage Encounter weekend, he began a daily personal or scriptural dialogue with the Lord, and he carries on this practice today a considerable number of years later. In addition, he in time added to his regular schedule a 10–15 minute period of biblical reading each day. Moreover, in recent months, he has begun also to spend a few minutes daily with some spiritual book other than the Bible.

During vacations, of course, he alters the pattern of his living, but the dialogue, Scripture reading and brief study of spirituality normally find a place even in those leisurely, unstructured days. Here is his dialogue written at holiday time during a magnificent, but hot July morning.

Dearest Jesus,

Thank you, Brother Jesus, for still another magnificent day. Again I ask for a beautiful, pleasant, safe week for everyone. So far, Brother Jesus, it has been beautiful.

Dear Father, I put myself into your hands. I want to commit myself to you totally, dear Father, but must admit to being afraid. Why do I not trust? Your Will will be done whether I want it or not. Furthermore, I will be happiest, most fulfilled, and most contented insofar as my life is in line with your plan. I do believe that. Yet I fail to trust. I fear that you will not take adequate care of my needs and wants to be happy. I fear the demands you might make on me which might cause discomfort or pain.

What I ask, Brother Jesus, is to help me to open myself totally to our Father and to give myself to Him completely. I feel reluctant to do this, Brother Jesus, as though some strong but invisible bonds are holding me back. I feel like a dog on a leash. I can go just so far, but no further. Often I just don't want to move at all, and I don't. Sometimes I can move, and do, with no difficulty. But I feel restrained by my own self-imposed bonds, from going beyond safe limits.

Love *forever*,
Me

Another equally close clergy friend likewise uses writing or journal keeping as a regular feature of his prayer routine. He does not follow that Marriage Encounter daily personal or Scripture dialogue technique. Instead, each morning this priest takes his journal, a spiral notebook, and spends some portion of meditative prayer time noting there reflections upon the previous day.

He examines failures and negative experiences without dwelling excessively upon them, seeks to learn something from those falls or hurts, and writes down these thoughts with appropriate expressions of repentance, conversion and hope. He then moves to victories and positive events, searching for lessons to be learned and inscribing his ponderings in the journal with suitable sentiments of praise, thanksgiving and petition.

My friends' two similar, but different methods of writing down their inner reflections help to surface and clarify interior thoughts and attitudes.

However, the journal system, followed faithfully and reviewed regularly, also can reveal trends in our inner lives. It will recall experiences keenly felt and highly influential at the time, but since forgotten. It may help us to avoid repetitive mistakes and encourage us when temporary setbacks cause us to lose perspective.

Those who make the extended Ignatian thirty day retreat or even an abbreviated eight day version use journal keeping for precisely this purpose—to record the reflections which emerge during their many prayer periods. They are thus not lost, manifest developing patterns, and, in ensuing months, can be reread with profit.

A religious sister colleague of mine concluded her sabbatical year of study in spirituality with such a thirty day retreat at Guelph, Ontario, Canada. Participants there make, under the guidance of a trained director, five hour-long meditations each day, including one in the middle of the night. After every period, however, they in addition take 10–20 minutes to write down their reflections, sharing them to the extent they choose at a daily meeting with the director. The content of those written down recollections serves as a springboard for suggestions to be followed during the day ahead.

We think of Pope John XXIII as "Good Pope John," the visionary convener of the Second Vatican Council, the friendly, heavy-set, jovial, open and elderly man surprisingly selected as the Holy Father for an "interim period." Photographers even once captured a picture of him as a papal diplomat with champagne glass in one hand and cigarette holder in the other.

But his personal diaries, published under the title *Journal of a Soul*, which were written almost without a break across sixty-seven years from his days as an eager seminarian of fourteen until six months prior to his death in 1963, disclose a quite different dimension of the beloved man. They show us a person intensely concerned about his relationship with the Lord and "reveal his intimate spiritual thoughts from the immaturity of adolescence, through the seminary, priesthood and ensuing years of difficult assignments, on through years as a papal diplomat in Bulgaria, Turkey and France and as Patriarch of Venice to the Papacy itself."[1]

The following entries in his journal were made while he was a young seminary student at Bergamo in 1898. They reflect his serious, introspective, prayerful and conscientious temperament at that age.

2 November, Wednesday

I must reproach myself with having wasted time, and with not having had recourse to frequent invocations. I must also take care not to give way to sleep during meditation as I did this morning. O Jesus, have mercy on me and grant peace to the dead.

3 November, Thursday

Today was spent travelling, and so it was as usual. Worst of all, sometimes I showed a little resentment in my words when I thought I was not being treated with sufficient consideration . . . and all this is pride, pride of the first water. And there were hardly any invocations. O God, pity me, for I do want to love you.

Tomorrow is the first Friday of the month and so a day of reparation to the Sacred Heart. Ah, if my own were a real reparation for my offenses! O Jesus, why should it not be so, if you come to my help?

4 November, Friday

A little better than yesterday, although my thoughts still wandered very much during Communion, and a little during the rosary, which proves I need to acquire the spirit of recollection, especially in the morning. I will use recollection also to obtain, as far as lies in my power, that mildness of manner which I sometimes lack and which is nevertheless most necessary if I am to increase in virtue and do much good to souls. O Jesus, O Mary, O St. Charles.[2]

This excerpt from an entry over sixty years later was made while Angelo Roncalli, now Pope John XXIII, was on retreat in the Vatican during the first part of his papacy:

Since the Lord chose me, unworthy as I am, for this great service, I feel I have no longer any special ties in this life, no family, no earthly country or nation, nor any particular preferences with regard to studies or projects, even good ones. Now, more than ever, I see myself only as the humble and unworthy "servant of God and servant of the servants of God." The whole world is my family. This sense of belonging to everyone must give character and vigor to my mind, my heart and my actions.

This vision, this feeling of belonging to the whole world, will give a new impulse to my constant and continual daily prayer: the Breviary, Holy Mass, the whole rosary and my faithful visits to Jesus in the tabernacle, all varied and ritual forms of close and trustful union with Jesus.

The experience of this first year gives me light and

strength in my efforts to straighten, to reform, and tactfully and patiently to make improvements in everything.

Above all, I am grateful to the Lord for the temperament he has given me, which preserves me from anxieties and tiresome perplexities. I feel I am under obedience in all things and I have noticed that this disposition, in great things and in small, gives me, unworthy as I am, a strength of daring simplicity, so wholly evangelical in its nature that it demands and obtains universal respect and edifies many. "Lord, I am not worthy. O Lord, be always my strength and the joy of my heart. My God, my mercy."[3]

In the next year, 1960, Pope John XXIII entered these words in his journal, comments which accurately mirrored how we observed the Holy Father's last years of life on earth.

I consider it a sign of great mercy shown me by the Lord Jesus that he continues to give me his peace, and even exterior signs of grace which, I am told, explain the imperturbable serenity that enables me to enjoy, in every hour of my day, a simplicity and meekness of soul that keep me ready to leave all at a moment's notice and depart for eternal life.

My failings and incapacities, and my "countless sins, offenses and negligences" for which I offer my daily Mass, are a cause of constant interior mortification, which prevents me from indulging in any kind of self-glorification, but does not weaken my confidence and trust in God, whose caressing hand I feel upon me, sustaining and encouraging.

At the beginning of my eightieth year it is all-important for me to humble myself and lose myself in the Lord, trusting that in his mercy he will open for me the gate to eternal life. Jesus, Mary, Joseph, may I breathe forth my soul in peace with you![4]

Journal keeping clearly, therefore, has a past and present tradition in the Church as a valued way of growing in the likeness of Christ and a helpful method of praying. But like all the methods in this section of *Behind Closed Doors*, it is but one way and neither indispensable nor more effective than other approaches. Moreover, we are not obliged to be trained in journal keeping nor must we observe any particular system in making our entries.

We have in this chapter sketched how several people have employed journals in diverse ways as part of their personal prayer lives. Nevertheless, if someone seeks more detailed explanation, specific direction and practical guidance for journal keeping, an inexpensive set of booklets by George F. Simons will provide those elements.

Journal for Life: Discovering Faith and Values through Journal Keeping is a two volume publication. Part I is entitled "Foundations" and Part II, "Theology from Experience."[5] They explain the purpose and worth of keeping a journal, give pragmatic steps for deriving maximum benefit from one, and supply several exercises to facilitate or deepen the writing process.

His practical summary of journal keeping taken from Volume I which follows below may whet the reader's appetite a bit and encourage a further exploration of this method.

The journal is a tool for personal spiritual growth. It functions by allowing you to get both an overall picture of yourself, your rhythms and directions, and insights into the specific events and feelings of your daily existence. It combines in itself the functions of many traditional religious exercises formerly contained in the examination of conscience, meditation, and spiritual direction.

To start your journal, obtain for yourself a notebook, preferably an unmarked, bound manuscript book. A bound book encourages you to keep mistakes or unpleasant entries. Uncomfortable parts of yourself which emerge need to be accepted and dealt with as a part of the whole picture. It should not be too easy to throw them away. An unmarked, unlined book enables you to establish personal boundaries and style without constraints of time and space generally found in diaries.

The journal is essentially *personal* and private, a mirror in which to see yourself. Never allow yourself to be pressured into revealing its contents, although, on the other hand, you may profit from choosing at times to share from it with other trusted individuals. Personal rereading is important, perhaps the entire week at the end of the week, the month at the end of the month, later on an annual rereading, etc.

Things which your journal might contain:

(a) a record of significant daily events and the personal feelings which accompanied or resulted from them. Graphic description of events and specific feelings should be emphasized rather than interpretations of what happened or what one thought the meanings of one's feelings were. Avoid the tendency to "philosophize." If a concrete record of events and feelings is missing, you will soon lose touch with what actually took place. Much potential self-understanding will be lost.

(b) dreams (night or day fantasies), again with as much detail as can be remembered. They will be more immediate if written in the present tense, e.g., "I dream that I am (rather than "I was") standing in a large room. My mother enters. She is wearing a flowered hat, etc."

(c) cut-outs or drawings of pictures or symbols which have particularly strong impact on you.

(d) fragments of usually forgotten personal history. Little pieces of memory which step into the light for a moment. Note the context in which they occur and the feelings which call them forth or result from them.

(e) the exercises which follow in this book. The journal serves as the workbook and repository in which these strategies are used. The instructions accompanying each exercise suggest the appropriate time for each to be used and indicate how the exercise might be adapted and repeated.

(f) anything you choose—but, again, try to be immediate and specific.

If convenient, your journal might accompany you throughout the day. Jottings made when experiences and feelings are vivid are more useful than those distilled by time. On the other hand, taking a certain time to write in the journal can serve as a meditation, a time in which images, feelings and concerns are allowed to move freely through the consciousness into the record.[6]

Journal keeping is a form of prayer. However, it also transcends the six methods of prayer described in this section and all those other ways of being present with God not included here. Regularly maintaining a personal journal could, consequently, serve as a link or an integrating vehicle bringing together the diverse efforts we make each day to pray. It can help us see more clearly where we have been, where we are and where we are heading in our journey to walk, talk and, ultimately, be with Christ the Lord.

Helpful Resources

Journal for Life: Discovering Faith and Values through Journal Keeping. George F. Simons. Volume I: "Foundations."

Journal for Life: Discovering Faith and Values through Journal Keeping. George F. Simons. Volume II: "Theology from Experience."
This two volume set is available as a set for $3.90 from ACTA Foundation, 4848 North Clark Street, Chicago, Illinois 60640.

Notes

Part I: Seven General Principles of Prayer

Principle #1: Constant Prayer, Silence and Solitude

1. Henri Nouwen, *Clowning in Rome*. Garden City, New York: Image Books, A Division of Doubleday and Company, 1979, pp. 61–62.
2. *Ibid.*, p. 76.
3. Fulton J. Sheen, *Treasure in Clay*. Garden City, New York: Doubleday and Company, 1980, pp. 190–191.
4. David Wilkerson, *The Cross and the Switchblade*. Old Tappan, New Jersey: Fleming H. Revell Company, 1963, p. 11.
5. *Ibid.*, p. 12.
6. Henri Nouwen, *The Way of the Heart*. New York: The Seabury Press, 1981, p. 31.

Principle #2: Being Present, Speaking and Listening to the Lord

1. John Killinger, *Prayer: The Act of Being with God*. Waco, Texas: Word Books, 1981, p. 16.
2. *The Priest and Stress*, issued by "The Bishops' Committee on Priestly Life and Ministry." Washington, D.C.: Office of Publishing Services, U.S. Catholic Conference, 1982, p. 18.
3. Killinger, *op. cit.*, pp. 14–15.
4. *Collegeville Bible Commentary*. "The Gospel According to Matthew." Commentary by Daniel J. Harrington, S.J. Collegeville, Minnesota: The Liturgical Press, 1983, p. 32.
5. "Circular Letter Concerning Some of the More Urgent Aspects of Spiritual Formation in Seminaries." Vatican Congregation for Catholic Education. January 6, 1980. Cf. "Origins," National Catholic News Service, Washington, D.C., Vol. 9, No. 38, March 6, 1980, p. 616.
6. Killinger, *op. cit.*, pp. 27–28.
7. Sheen, *op. cit.*, p. 194.
8. M. Basil Pennington, *Centering Prayer*. Garden City, N.Y.: Doubleday and Company, 1980, pp. 48–49.
9. *Ibid.*, p. 47.

10. George Maloney, S.J., *Prayer of the Heart*. Notre Dame, Indiana: Ave Maria Press, 1981, pp. 149–150.

11. *Ibid.*, pp. 150, 140.

12. Pennington, *op. cit.*, pp. 171–177. Chapter XII, "Relax!" includes detailed descriptions of several techniques for such relaxation preparing for prayer.

13. Maloney, *op. cit.*, p. 140.

Principle #3: Different Ways of Praying

1. Killinger, *op. cit.*, Table of Contents.

Principle #4: Prayer and Faith

1. Webster's Third New International Dictionary. Springfield, Mass.: G. and C. Merriam Co., Publishers, 1976, p. 816.

2. *The New World Dictionary—Concordance to the New American Bible*. New York: World Publishing, 1970, p. 183.

3. Henri J.M. Nouwen. *In Mei Memoriam*. Notre Dame, Indiana: Ave Maria Press, 1980.

4. *Ibid.*, p. 24.

5. Henri J.M. Nouwen. *A Letter of Consolation*. San Francisco: Harper and Row, 1982, pp. 63–64.

6. Nouwen. *In Mei Memoriam, op. cit.*, p. 23.

7. *Ibid.*, p. 24.

8. *Ibid.*, pp. 30–31; 32.

9. *Ibid.*, p. 27.

10. *Ibid.*, p. 27.

11. *Ibid.*, pp. 27–28.

12. *Music in Catholic Worship*. Issued by the Bishops' Committee on the Liturgy, National Conference of Catholic Bishops. Washington, D.C.: United States Catholic Conference, 1983 (Revised Edition), p. 9.

13. *Vatican Council II*, "Constitution on the Sacred Liturgy." Edited by Austin Flannery, O.P. Northport, N.Y.: Costello Publishing Company, 1975, pp. 4–5, article 7.

Principle #5: Prayer and Feelings

1. *Ibid.*, pp. 161–163.

2. *Music in Catholic Worship, op. cit.*, p. 9.

3. *Ibid.*, p. 9.

Principle #6:   Dry and Dark Periods of Prayer

1. R. Garrigou-LaGrange, O.P., *The Three Ages of the Interior Life.* St. Louis: B. Herder Book Co., 1951, Volume I, p. vi. This two volume classic is a comprehensive treatment of the spiritual life with particular emphasis on the teaching of St. Thomas Aquinas, St. John of the Cross and St. Francis de Sales. While an older book and thus in need of some updating, it nevertheless contains considerable ageless wisdom on the inner life. I am using it as the basis for my treatment of the three stages and the two passive purifications.

2. *Ibid.*, Volume I, p. 190.

3. *Ibid.*, Volume II, p. 655.

4. *Ibid.*, Volume I, pp. 190–191.

5. *Ibid*, p. 191.

6. *Ibid.*, p. 190.

7. *Ibid.*, pp. 192–193.

8. *Ibid.*, p. 188.

9. Daniel Yankelovich, *New Rules: Searching for Self-Fulfillment in a World Turned Upside Down.* New York: Random House, 1981, p. 81.

10. *Ibid.*, pp. 8–9.

11. *Ibid.*, p. 5.

12. *Ibid.*, p. 78.

13. *Ibid.*, p. 59.

14. Gavan Daws, *Holy Man: Father Damien of Molokai.* New York: Harper and Row, 1973, p. 158.

15. *Ibid.*, p. 159.

16. *Ibid.*, pp. 159–160

17. *Ibid.*, p. 186.

Principle #7:   Cross Stamped Prayer

1. James J. DiGiacomo, S.J. "Teaching the Next New Breed." *America*, June 27, 1981, pp. 519–520.

2. *Ibid.*, p. 520.

3. *Ibid.*, pp. 521–522.

4. Dr. Frederick J. Parrella. "A Tale of Two Sundays: Liturgical Reform Gone Astray." *The Christian Century*, October 7, 1981, p. 993.

5. *Ibid.*, p. 992.

6. *Ibid.*

7. Leonard Foley, O.F.M. *Saint of the Day.* Cincinnati: St. Anthony Messenger Press, 1975, Volume II, pp. 102–107.

8. *Ibid.,* Volume I, pp. 5–7

9. *Ibid.,* Volume II, pp. 100–102.

10. Boniface Harvey, O.F.M., *No Greater Love.* Notre Dame, Indiana: Ave Maria Press, 1982, pp. 69–70.

11. Mother Teresa, *Words To Love By.* Notre Dame, Indiana: Ave Maria Press, 1983, p. 6.

12. *Ibid.,* p. 8.

13. *Vatican Council II, op. cit.,* pp. 10–11, articles 26–27.

14. *Ibid.,* p. 1, article 2.

Part II: Seven Different Ways of Praying

Method #1: Mary and the Rosary

1. Mary Dunn, "Why Young Catholics Leave the Church—and Return." *Catholic Twin Circle,* January 10, 1982, p. 20.

2. Mary Gordon, "Coming to Terms with Mary." *Commonweal,* January 15, 1982, p. 14.

3. Sally Cuneen, "The Liberation of Mary." *Notre Dame Magazine,* December, 1981, p. 11.

4. Mitch Finley, "Recovering the Rosary." *America,* May 7, 1983, p. 351.

5. Mary McDonough, "Letters." *America,* June 11, 1983, p. 466.

6. Rev. Allan Hawkins, "Letters." *America,* June 11, 1983, p. 466.

7. Eamon R. Carroll, O. Carm., "Woman of Faith." *Emmanuel,* May 1983, pp. 185–186.

8. *Vatican Council II, op. cit.,* pp. 421–422, article 67.

9. National Conference of Catholic Bishops, *Behold Your Mother: Woman of Faith.* Washington: United States Catholic Conference, 1973.

10. Pope Paul VI, *Devotion to the Blessed Virgin Mary.* Washington: United States Catholic Conference, 1974.

11. *Scriptural Rosary.* Chicago: Christianica Center, 6 North Michigan Avenue, Chicago, Illinois 60602, 1980, pp. 9–17.

12. Robert C. Broderick, "Pray the Rosary." St. Paul: The Leaflet Missal Company, 419 W. Minnehaha Avenue, St. Paul, Minnesota 55102, p. 2.

13. Mitch Finley, *op. cit.,* p. 351.

14. Pope Paul VI, *op. cit.,* pp. 35–36.

15. *Ibid.*, p. 34.
16. *Ibid.*, p. 32.
17. *Ibid.*, p. 33.
18. Mitch Finley, *op. cit.*, p. 351.
19. Pope Paul VI, *op. cit.*, p. 36.
20. National Conference of Catholic Bishops, *Behold Your Mother*, *op. cit.*, pp. 36–37.

Method #2: The Church's Official Prayer Book

1. Roland E. Murphy, O. Carm., "Psalms." *The Jerome Biblical Commentary.* Englewood Cliffs, New Jersey: Prentice-Hall, Inc., 1968, p. 598.
2. *The New Testament.* Confraternity of Christian Doctrine Edition. Paterson, New Jersey: St. Anthony Guild Press, 1941, pp. 315–316.
3. A.M. Roguet, O.P., *The Liturgy of the Hours.* Collegeville, Minnesota: The Liturgical Press, 1971, pp. 91–92.
4. *Vatican Council II*, *op. cit.*, Chapter IV, articles 87–100.
5. Roguet, *op. cit.*, pp. 81–82.
6. *Vatican Council II*, *op. cit.*, articles 83–86.
7. *Ibid.*, article 100.

Method #3: Reflective Biblical Reading

1. *Vatican Council II*, *op. cit.*, "Dogmatic Constitution on Divine Revelation," article 11.
2. *Ibid.*, article 25.
3. *Ibid.*
4. *Vatican Council II*, *op. cit.*, "Constitution on the Sacred Liturgy," article 24.
5. George Martin, *Reading Scripture as the Word of God.* South Bend, Indiana; Servant Books, 1975, p. 9.
6. *Ibid.*, p. 8.
7. *Ibid.*
8. *Ibid.*
9. *Ibid.*, pp. 63–64.

Method #4: Meditation

1. *Time*, June 6, 1983, p. 50.
2. *Ibid.*, p. 52.

3. J. Murray Elwood, *A Month with Christ*. Notre Dame, Indiana: Ave Maria Press, 1979.

4. *Ibid.*, pp. 6–9.

5. Henri J.M. Nouwen, *Clowning in Rome, op. cit.*, p. 76.

6. *Ibid.*, pp. 79–81.

7. Leonard Foley, O.F.M., *Saint of the Day*. Cincinnati, Ohio; St. Anthony Messenger Press, 1975. Two volume paperback; single volume hardcover.

Method #5: Charismatic and Healing Prayer

1. Edward D. O'Connor, C.S.C., *The Pentecostal Movement in the Catholic Church*. Notre Dame, Indiana: Ave Maria Press, 1971, pp. 13–18.

2. Leon Joseph Cardinal Suenens, *A New Pentecost?* New York: The Seabury Press, 1975, pp. 74–75.

3. O'Connor, *op. cit.*, p. 18.

4. Suenens, *op. cit.*, p. 75.

5. *Ibid.*, p. 68.

6. *Ibid.*, p. 97.

7. *Ibid.*, p. 102.

8. O'Connor, *op. cit.*, pp. 292–293.

9. Suenens, *op. cit.*, p. 94.

10. Dennis and Matthew Linn, S.J., *Healing Life's Hurts*. New York: Paulist Press, 1978; Francis MacNutt, *Healing*. Notre Dame, Indiana: Ave Maria Press, 1974; Francis MacNutt, *The Power To Heal*. Notre Dame, Indiana: Ave Maria Press, 1977; Barbara Shlemon, *To Heal as Jesus Healed*. Notre Dame, Indiana: Ave Maria Press, 1978; Barbara Shlemon, *Healing Prayer*. Notre Dame, Indiana: Ave Maria Press, 1976.

11. Francis MacNutt, *The Prayer That Heals: Praying for Healing in the Family*. Notre Dame, Indiana: Ave Maria Press, 1981, pp. 45–47.

Method #6: Centering Prayer

1. *Time*. June 6, 1983, pp. 52–53.

2. M. Basil Pennington, O.C.S.O., *Centering Prayer: Reviewing an Ancient Christian Prayer Form*. Garden City, New York: Doubleday and Company, Inc., 1980.

3. *Ibid.*, p. 2.

4. *Ibid.*, p. 48.

5. *Ibid.*

6. *Ibid.*, p. 45.
7. *Ibid.*, p. 50.
8. *Ibid.*, p. 61.
9. *Ibid.*, p. 45.
10. *Ibid.*, p. 42.
11. *Ibid.*, p. 45.
12. *Ibid.*, pp. 54–55.
13. *Ibid.*, p. 45.
14. *Ibid.*, p. 56.
15. *Ibid.*, pp. 57–59.
16. *Ibid.*, p. 60.

Method #7: Journal Keeping

1. Pope John XXIII, *Journal of a Soul.* New York: McGraw-Hill Book Company, 1964, cover jacket.
2. *Ibid.*, p. 54.
3. *Ibid.*, pp. 298–299.
4. *Ibid.*, p. 301.
5. George F. Simons, *Journal for Life.* Chicago: ACTA Foundation, Volume I, 1975; Volume II, 1977.
6. *Ibid.*, Volume I, pp. 17–18.

The Church's Official Prayer Book

General Instruction for the
Liturgy of the Hours (Chapters 1–3)

The Liturgy of the Hours, the Church's official prayer book, contains like the other renewed liturgical texts an explanatory introduction. This instruction describes in detail the structure of the divine office and gives specific rules or rubrics for its actual use. However, the introduction also includes a succinct, yet rich treatise on prayer. Excerpts from the instruction, not widely available on the popular level, are included here as a valuable resource item. The reader might quickly review Chapter 2 in Part II for some practical suggestions on how to derive the most benefit from this preface to the Liturgy of the Hours.

.

Importance of the Liturgy of the Hours or Divine Office in the Life of the Church

1.   Public and common prayer by the people of God is rightly considered to be among the primary duties of the Church. From the very beginning those who were baptized "devoted themselves to the teaching of the apostles and to the community, to the breaking of the bread, and to prayer" (Acts 2:42). The Acts of the Apostles gives frequent testimony to the fact that the Christian community prayed with one accord.[1]

The witness of the early Church teaches us that individual Christians devoted themselves to prayer at fixed times. Then, in different places, it soon became the established practice to assign special times for common prayer, for example, the last hour of the day when evening draws on and the lamp is lighted, or the first hour when night draws to a close with the rising of the sun.

In the course of time other hours came to be sanctified by prayer in common. These were seen by the Fathers as foreshadowed in the Acts of the Apostles. There we read of the disciples gathered together at the third hour.[2] The prince of the apostles "went up on the housetop to pray, about the sixth hour" (10:9); "Peter and John were going up to the temple at the hour of prayer, the ninth hour" (3:1); "about midnight Paul and Silas were praying and singing hymns to God" (16:25).

2.   Such prayer in common gradually took the form of a set cycle of hours. This liturgy of the hours or divine office, enriched by readings, is principally a prayer of praise and petition. Indeed, it is the prayer of the Church with Christ and to Christ.

I. PRAYER OF CHRIST

CHRIST THE INTERCESSOR WITH THE FATHER

3.   When the Word, proceeding from the Father as the splendor of his glory, came to give us all a share in God's life, "Christ Jesus, High Priest

of the new and eternal covenant, taking human nature, introduced into this earthly exile the hymn of praise that is sung throughout all ages in the halls of heaven."[3] From then on in Christ's heart the praise of God assumes a human sound in words of adoration, expiation, and intercession, presented to the Father by the Head of the new humanity, the Mediator between God and his people, in the name of all and for the good of all.

4.   In his goodness the Son of God, who is one with his Father (see Jn 10:30) and who on entering the world said: "Here I am! I come, God, to do your will" (Heb 10:9; see Jn 6:38), has left us the lesson of his own prayer. The Gospels many times show us Christ at prayer: when his mission is revealed by the Father;[4] before he calls the apostles;[5] when he blesses God at the multiplication of the loaves;[6] when he is transfigured on the mountain;[7] when he heals the deaf-mute;[8] when he raises Lazarus;[9] before he asks for Peter's confession of faith;[10] when he teaches the disciples how to pray;[11] when the disciples return from their mission;[12] when he blesses the little children;[13] when he prays for Peter.[14]

The work of each day was closely bound up with his prayer, indeed flowed out from it: he would retire into the desert or into the hills to pray,[15] rise very early[16] or spend the night up to the fourth watch[17] in prayer to God.[18]

We are right in thinking that he took part both in public prayers: in the synagogues, which he entered on the Sabbath "as his custom was;"[19] in the temple, which he called a house of prayer;[20] and in the private prayers that for devout Israelites were a daily practice. He used the traditional blessings of God at meals, as is expressly mentioned in connection with the multiplication of the loaves,[21] the last supper,[22] and the meal at Emmaus.[23] He also joined with the disciples in a hymn of praise.[24]

To the very end of his life, as his passion was approaching,[25] at the last supper,[26] in the agony in the garden,[27] and on the cross,[28] the divine teacher showed that prayer was the soul of his Messianic ministry and paschal death. "In the days of his life on earth he offered up prayers and entreaties with loud cries and tears to the one who could deliver him from death and because of his reverence his prayer was heard" (Heb 5:7). By a single offering on the altar of the cross "he has made perfect forever those who are being sanctified" (Heb 10–14). Raised from the dead, he lives for ever, making intercession for us.[29]

II. PRAYER OF THE CHURCH

COMMANDMENT TO PRAY

5.   Jesus has commanded us to do as he did. On many occasions he said: "Pray," "ask," "seek"[30] "in my name."[31] He taught us how to pray in what is known as the Lord's Prayer.[32] He taught us that prayer is necessary,[33] that it should be humble,[34] watchful,[35] persevering, confident in the Father's goodness,[36] single-minded, and in conformity with God's nature.[37]

Here and there in their letters the apostles have handed on to us many prayers, particularly of praise and thanks. They instruct us on prayer in the Holy Spirit,[38] through Christ,[39] offered to God,[40] as to its persistence and constancy,[41] its power to sanctify,[42] and on prayer of praise,[43] thanks,[44] petition,[45] and intercession for all.[46]

CHRIST'S PRAYER CONTINUED BY THE CHURCH

6.   Since we are entirely dependent on God, we must acknowledge and express this sovereignty of the Creator, as the devout people of every age have done by means of prayer.

Prayer directed to God must be linked with Christ, the Lord of all, the one Mediator[47] through whom alone we have access to God.[48] He unites to himself the whole human community[49] in such a way that there is an intimate bond between the prayer of Christ and the prayer of all humanity. In Christ and in Christ alone human worship of God receives its redemptive value and attains its goal.

7.   There is a special and very close bond between Christ and those whom he makes members of his Body, the Church, through the sacrament of rebirth. Thus, from the Head all the riches belonging to the Son flow throughout the whole Body: the communication of the Spirit, the truth, the life, and the participation in the divine sonship that Christ manifested in all his prayer when he dwelt among us.

Christ's priesthood is also shared by the whole Body of the Church, so that the baptized are consecrated as a spiritual temple and holy priesthood through the rebirth of baptism and the anointing by the Holy Spirit[50] and are empowered to offer the worship of the New Covenant, a worship that derives not from our own powers but from Christ's merit and gift.

"God could give us no greater gift than to establish as our Head the Word through whom he created all things and to unite us to that Head as members. The results are many. The Head is Son of God and Son of Man, one as God with the Father and one as man with us. When we speak in prayer to the Father, we do not separate the Son from him and when the Son's Body prays it does not separate itself from its Head. It is the one Savior of his Body, the Lord Christ Jesus, who prays for us and in us and who is prayed to by us. He prays for us as our priest, in us as our Head; he is prayed to by us as our God. Recognize therefore our own voice in him and his voice in us."[51]

The excellence of Christian prayer lies in its sharing in the reverent love of the only-begotten Son for the Father and in the prayer that the Son put into words in his earthly life and that still continues without ceasing in the name of the whole human race and for its salvation, throughout the universal Church and in all its members.

ACTION OF THE HOLY SPIRIT

8.   The unity of the Church at prayer is brought about by the Holy Spirit, who is the same in Christ,[52] in the whole Church, and in every baptized person. It is this Spirit who "helps us in our weakness" and "intercedes for us with longings too deep for words" (Rom 8:26). As the Spirit of the Son, he gives us "the spirit of adopted children, by which we cry out: Abba, Father" (Rom 8:15; see Gal 4:6; 1 Cor 12:3; Eph 5:18; Jude 20). There can be therefore no Christian prayer without the action of the Holy Spirit, who unites the whole Church and leads it through the Son to the Father.

COMMUNITY CHARACTER OF PRAYER

9.   It follows that the example and precept of our Lord and the apostles in regard to constant and persevering prayer are not to be seen as a purely legal regulation. They belong to the very essence of the Church itself, which is a community and which in prayer must express its nature as a community. Hence, when the community of believers is first mentioned in the Acts of the Apostles, it is seen as a community gathered together at prayer "with the women and Mary, the mother of Jesus, and his brothers" (Acts 1:14). "There was one heart and soul in the company of those who believed" (Acts 4:32). Their oneness in spirit was founded on the word of God, on the communion of charity, on prayer, and on the eucharist.[53]

Though prayer in private and in seclusion[54] is always necessary and to be encouraged[55] and is practiced by the members of the Church through Christ in the Holy Spirit, there is a special excellence in the prayer of the community. Christ himself has said: "Where two or three are gathered together in my name, I am there in their midst" (Mt 18:20).

III. LITURGY OF THE HOURS

CONSECRATION OF TIME

10.   Christ taught us: "You must pray at all times and not lose heart" (Lk 18:1). The Church has been faithful in obeying this instruction; it never ceases to offer prayer and makes this exhortation its own: "Through him (Jesus) let us offer to God an unceasing sacrifice of praise" (Heb 15:15). The Church fulfills this precept not only by celebrating the eucharist but in other ways also, especially through the liturgy of the hours. By ancient Christian tradition what distinguishes the liturgy of the hours from other liturgical services is that it consecrates to God the whole cycle of the day and the night.[56]

11.   The purpose of the liturgy of the hours is to sanctify the day and the whole range of human activity. Therefore its structure has been revised in such a way as to make each hour once more correspond as nearly as possible to natural time and to take account of the circumstances of life today.[57]

Hence, "that the day may be truly sanctified and the hours themselves recited with spiritual advantage, it is best that each of them be prayed at a time most closely corresponding to the true time of each canonical hour."[58]

LITURGY OF THE HOURS AND THE EUCHARIST

12.   To the different hours of the day the liturgy of the hours extends[59] the praise and thanksgiving, the memorial of the mysteries of salvation, the petitions and the foretaste of heavenly glory that are present in the eucharist mystery, "the center and high point in the whole life of the Christian community."[60]

The liturgy of the hours is in turn an excellent preparation for the celebration of the eucharist itself, for it inspires and deepens in a fitting way the dispositions necessary for the fruitful celebration of the eucharist: faith, hope, love, devotion, and the spirit of self-denial.

PRIESTHOOD OF CHRIST IN THE LITURGY OF THE HOURS

13.   In the Holy Spirit Christ carries out through the Church "the task of redeeming humanity and giving perfect Glory to God,"[61] not only when the eucharist is celebrated and the sacraments administered but also in other ways and especially when the liturgy of the hours is celebrated.[62] There Christ himself is present—in the gathered community, in the proclamation of God's word, "in the prayer and song of the Church."[63]

SANCTIFICATION OF GOD'S PEOPLE

14.   Our sanctification is accomplished[64] and worship is offered to God in the liturgy of the hours in such a way that an exchange or dialogue is set up between God and us, in which "God is speaking to his people . . . and his people are responding to him by both song and prayer."[65]

Those taking part in the liturgy of the hours have access to holiness of the richest kind through the life-giving word of God, which in this liturgy receives great emphasis. Thus its readings are drawn from sacred Scripture, God's words in the psalms are sung in his presence, and the intercessions, prayers, and hymns are inspired by Scripture and steeped in its spirit.[66]

Hence, not only when those things are read "that are written for our instruction" (Rom 15:4), but also when the Church prays or sings, faith is deepened for those who take part and their minds are lifted up to God, in order to offer him their worship as intelligent beings and to receive his grace more plentifully.[67]

PRAISING GOD WITH THE CHURCH IN HEAVEN

15.   In the liturgy of the hours the Church exercises the priestly office of its Head and offers to God "without ceasing"[68] a sacrifice of praise, that is, a tribute of lips acknowledging his name.[69] This prayer is "the voice of a bride addressing her bridegroom; it is the very prayer that Christ himself, together with his Body, addresses to the Father."[70] "All who render this service are not only fulfilling a duty of the Church, but also are sharing in the greatest honor of Christ's Bride for by offering these praises to God they are standing before God's throne in the name of the Church, their Mother."[71]

16.   When the Church offers praise to God in the liturgy of the hours, it unites itself with that hymn of praise sung throughout all ages in the

halls of heaven;[72] it also receives a foretaste of the song of praise in heaven, described by John in the Book of Revelation, the song sung continually before the throne of God and of the Lamb. Our close union with the Church in heaven is given effective voice "when we all, from every tribe and tongue and people and nation redeemed by Christ's blood (see Rv 5:9) and gathered together into the one Church, glorify the triune God with one hymn of praise."[73]

The prophets came almost to a vision of this liturgy of heaven as the victory of a day without night, of a light without darkness: "The sun will no more be your light by day, and the brightness of the moon will not shine upon you, but the Lord will be your everlasting light" (Is 60:19; see Rv 21:23 and 25). "There will be a single day, known to the Lord, not day and night, and at evening there will be light" (Zech 14:7). Already "the end of the ages has come upon us (see 1 Cor 10:11) and the renewal of the world has been irrevocably established and in a true sense is being anticipated in this world."[74] By faith we too are taught the meaning of our temporal life, so that we look forward with all creation to the revealing of God's children.[75] In the liturgy of the hours we proclaim this faith, we express and nourish this hope, we share in some degree the joy of everlasting praise and of that day that knows no setting.

PETITION AND INTERCESSION

17.   But besides the praise of God, the Church in the liturgy of the hours expresses the prayers and desires of all the faithful; indeed, it prays to Christ, and through him to the Father, for the salvation of the whole world.[76] The Church's voice is not just its own; it is also Christ's voice, since its prayers are offered in Christ's name, that is, "through our Lord Jesus Christ," and so the Church continues to offer the prayer and petition that Christ poured out in the days of his earthly life[77] and that have therefore a unique effectiveness. The ecclesial community thus exercises a truly maternal function in bringing souls to Christ, not only by charity, good example, and works of penance but also by prayer.[78]

The concern with prayer involves those especially who have been called by a special mandate to carry out the liturgy of the hours: bishops and priests as they pray in virtue of their office for their own people and for the whole people of God;[79] other sacred ministers, and also religious.[80]

18.   Those then who take part in the liturgy of the hours bring growth to God's people in a hidden but fruitful apostolate,[81] for the work of the apostolate is directed to this end, "that all who are made children of God

by faith and baptism should come together to praise God in the midst of this Church, to take part in the sacrifice, and to eat the Lord's Supper."[82]

Thus by their lives the faithful show forth and reveal to others "the mystery of Christ and the real nature of the true Church. It is of the essence of the Church to be visible yet endowed with invisible resources, eager to act yet intent on contemplation, present in this world yet not at home in it."[83]

In their turn the readings and prayers of the liturgy of the hours form a wellspring of the Christian life: the table of sacred Scripture and the writings of the saints nurture its life and prayers strengthen it. Only the Lord, without whom we can do nothing,[84] can, in response to our request, give power and increase to what we do,[85] so that we may be built up each day in the Spirit into the temple of God,[86] to the measure of Christ's fullness,[87] and receive greater strength also to bring the good news of Christ to those outside.[88]

HARMONY OF MIND AND VOICE

19.   Mind and voice must be in harmony in a celebration that is worthy, attentive, and devout, if this prayer is to be made their own by those taking part and to be a source of devotion, a means of gaining God's manifold grace, a deepening of personal prayer, and an incentive to the work of the apostolate.[89] All should be intent on cooperating with God's grace, so as not to receive it in vain. Seeking Christ, penetrating ever more deeply into his mystery through prayer[90] they should offer praise and petition to God with the same mind and heart as the divine Redeemer when he prayed.[R1]

IV. PARTICIPANTS IN THE LITURGY OF THE HOURS

A. Celebration in Common

20.   The liturgy of the hours, like other liturgical services, is not a private matter but belongs to the whole Body of the Church, whose life it both expresses and affects.[91] This liturgy stands out most strikingly as an ecclesial celebration when, through the bishop surrounded by his priests and ministers,[92] the local Church celebrates it. For "in the local Church the one, holy, catholic, and apostolic Church is truly present and at work."[93] Such a celebration is therefore most earnestly recommended.

When, in the absence of the bishop, a chapter of canons or other priests celebrate the liturgy of the hours, they should always respect the true time of day and, as far as possible, the people should take part. The same is to be said of collegiate chapters.

21.   Wherever possible, other groups of the faithful should celebrate the liturgy of the hours communally in church. This especially applies to parishes—the cells of the diocese, established under their pastors, taking the place of the bishop; they "represent in some degree the visible Church established throughout the world."[94]

22.   Hence, when the people are invited to the liturgy of the hours and come together in unity of heart and voice, they show forth the Church in its celebration of the mystery of Christ.[95]

23.   Those in holy orders or with a special canonical mission[96] have the responsibility of initiating and directing the prayer of the community; "they should expend every effort so that those entrusted to their care may become of one mind in prayer."[97] They must therefore see to it that the people are invited, and prepared by suitable instruction, to celebrate the principal hours in common, especially on Sundays and holydays.[98] They should teach the people how to make this participation a source of genuine prayer;[99] they should therefore give the people suitable guidance in the Christian understanding of the psalms, in order to progress by degrees to a greater appreciation and more frequent use of the prayer of the Church.[100]

24.   Communities of canons, monks, nuns, and other religious who celebrate the liturgy of the hours by rule or according to their constitutions, whether with the general rite or a particular rite, in whole or in part, represent in a special way the Church at prayer. They are a fuller sign of the Church as it continuously praises God with one voice and they fulfill the duty of "working," above all by prayer, "to build up and increase the whole Mystical Body of Christ, and for the good of the local Churches."[101] This is especially true of those living the contemplative life.

25.   Even when having no obligation to communal celebration, all sacred ministers and all clerics living in a community or meeting together should arrange to say at least some part of the liturgy of the hours in common, particularly morning prayer and evening prayer.[102]

26.   Men and women religious not bound to a common celebration, as well as members of any institute of perfection, are strongly urged to gather together, by themselves or with the people, to celebrate the liturgy of the hours or part of it.

27.   Lay groups gathering for prayer, apostolic work, or any other reason are encouraged to fulfill the Church's duty[103] by celebrating part of the liturgy of the hours. The laity must learn above all how in the liturgy they are adoring God the Father in spirit and in truth;[104] they should bear in mind that through public worship and prayer they reach all humanity and can contribute significantly to the salvation of the whole world.[105]

Finally, it is of great advantage for the family, the domestic sanctuary of the Church, not only to pray together to God but also to celebrate some parts of the liturgy of the hours as occasion offers, in order to enter more deeply into the life of the Church.[106]

B. Mandate to Celebrate the Liturgy of the Hours

28.   Sacred ministers have the liturgy of the hours entrusted to them in such a particular way that even when the faithful are not present they are to pray it themselves with the adaptations necessary under these circumstances. The Church commissions them to celebrate the liturgy of the hours so as to ensure at least in their persons the regular carrying out of the duty of the whole community and the unceasing continuance of Christ's prayer in the Church.[107]

The bishop represents Christ in an eminent and conspicuous way and is the high priest of his flock; the life in Christ of his faithful people may be said in a sense to derive from him and depend on him.[108] He should, then, be the first of all the members of his Church in offering prayer. His prayer in the recitation of the liturgy of the hours is always made in the name of the Church and on behalf of the Church entrusted to him.[109]

United as they are with the bishop and the whole presbyterium, priests are themselves representative in a special way of Christ the Priest[110] and so share the same responsibility of praying to God for the people entrusted to them and indeed for the whole world.[111]

All these ministers fulfill the ministry of the Good Shepherd who prays for his sheep that they may have life and so be brought into perfect unity.[112] In the liturgy of the hours that the Church sets before them they are not only to find a source of devotion and a strengthening of personal prayer,[113] but must also nourish and foster pastoral missionary activity as the fruit of their contemplation to gladden the whole Church of God.[114]

29.   Hence bishops, priests, and deacons aspiring to the priesthood, who have received from the Church the mandate to celebrate the liturgy of the hours (see no. 17), are bound by the obligation of reciting the full sequence of hours each day,[114] [(b)] observing as far as possible the true time of day.

They should, first and foremost, attach due importance to those hours that are, so to speak, the two hinges of the liturgy of the hours, that is, morning prayer and evening prayer, which should not be omitted except for a serious reason.

They should faithfully pray the office of readings, which is above all a liturgical celebration of the word of God. In this way they fulfill daily a duty that is peculiarly their own, that is, of receiving the word of God into their lives, so that they may become more perfect as disciples of the Lord and experience more deeply the unfathomable riches of Christ.[115]

In order to sanctify the whole day more completely, they will also treasure the recitation of daytime prayer and night prayer, to round off the whole *Opus Dei* and to commend themselves to God before retiring.

30.   Permanent deacons, to whom the mandate of the Church also applies, are to recite daily the part of the liturgy of the hours that has been determined by the conference of bishops.[116]

31.   a. Cathedral and collegiate chapters should celebrate in choir those parts of the liturgy of the hours that are prescribed for them by the general law or by particular law.

In private recitation individual members of these chapters should include those hours that are recited in their chapter,[R2] in addition to the hours prescribed for all sacred ministers.[117]

b. Religious communities bound to the recitation of the liturgy of the hours and their individual members should celebrate the hours in keeping with their own particular law; but the prescription of no. 29 in regard to those in holy orders is to be respected.

Communities bound to choir should celebrate the whole sequence of the hours daily in choir;[118] when absent from choir their members should recite the hours in keeping with their own particular law; but the prescriptions in no. 29 are always to be respected.

32.   Other religious communities and their individual members are advised to celebrate some parts of the liturgy of the hours, in accordance with their own situation, for it is the prayer of the Church that makes the whole Church, scattered throughout the world, one in heart and mind.[119]

This recommendation applies also to laypersons.[120]

C. Structure of the Celebration

33.   The structure of the liturgy of the hours follows laws of its own and incorporates in its own way elements found in other Christian celebrations. Thus it is so constructed that, after a hymn, there is always psalmody, then a long or short reading of sacred Scripture, and finally prayer of petition.

In a celebration in common and in private recitation the essential structure of this liturgy remains the same, that is, it is a conversation between God and his people. Celebration in common, however, expresses more clearly the ecclesial nature of the liturgy of the hours; it makes for active participation by all, in a way suited to each one's condition, through the acclamations, dialogue, alternating psalmody, and similar elements. It also better provides for the different literary genres that make up the liturgy of the hours.[121] Hence, whenever it is possible to have a celebration in common, with the people present and actively taking part, this kind of celebration is to be preferred to one that is individual and, as it were, private.[122] It is also advantageous to sing the office in choir and in community as opportunity offers, in accordance with the nature and function of the individual parts.

In this way the Apostle's exhortation is obeyed: "Let the word of Christ dwell in you in all its fullness, as you teach and counsel each other in all wisdom by psalms, hymns, and spiritual canticles, singing thankfully to God in your hearts" (Col 3:16; see Eph 5:19–20).

◊ *Chapter II*

Sanctification of the Day:
The Different Liturgical Hours

I. INTRODUCTION TO THE WHOLE OFFICE

34.   The whole office begins as a rule with an invitatory. This consists in the verse, *Lord, open my lips. And my mouth will proclaim your praise,* and Ps 95. This psalm invites the faithful each day to sing God's praise and to listen to his voice and draws them to hope for "the Lord's rest."[1]

In place of Ps 95, Ps 100, Ps 67, or Ps 24 may be used as circumstances may suggest.

It is preferable to recite the invitatory psalm responsorially as it is set out in the text, that is, with the antiphon recited at the beginning, then repeated, and repeated again after each strophe.

35.   The invitatory is placed at the beginning of the whole sequence of the day's prayer, that is, it precedes either morning prayer or the office of readings, whichever of these liturgical rites begins the day. The invitatory psalm with its antiphon may be omitted, however, when the invitatory is the prelude to morning prayer.

36.   The variation of the invitatory antiphon, to suit the different liturgical days, is indicated at its place of occurrence.

II. MORNING PRAYER AND EVENING PRAYER

37.   "By the venerable tradition of the universal Church, lauds as morning prayer and vespers as evening prayer are the two hinges on which the daily office turns; hence they are to be considered as the chief hours and celebrated as such."[2]

38.   As is clear from many of the elements that make it up, morning prayer is intended and arranged to sanctify the morning. St. Basil the

Great gives an excellent description of this character in these words: "It is said in the morning in order that the first stirrings of our mind and will may be consecrated to God and that we may take nothing in hand until we have been gladdened by the thought of God, as it is written: 'I was mindful of God and was glad' (Ps 77:4 [Jerome's translation from Hebrew]), or set our bodies to any task before we do what has been said: 'I will pray to you, Lord, you will hear my voice in the morning; I will stand before you in the morning and gaze on you' (Ps 5:4–5)."[3]

Celebrated as it is as the light of a new day is dawning, this hour also recalls the resurrection of the Lord Jesus, the true light enlightening all people (see Jn 1:9) and "the sun of justice" (Mal 4:2), "rising from on high" (Lk 1:78). Hence, we can well understand the advice of St. Cyprian: "There should be prayer in the morning so that the resurrection of the Lord may thus be celebrated."[4]

39.   When evening approaches and the day is already far spent, evening prayer is celebrated in order that "we may give thanks for what has been given us, or what we have done well, during the day."[5] We also recall the redemption through the prayer we send up "like incense in the Lord's sight," and in which "the raising up of our hands" becomes "an evening sacrifice."[6] This sacrifice "may also be interpreted more spiritually as the true evening sacrifice that our Savior the Lord entrusted to the apostles at supper on the evening when he instituted the sacred mysteries of the Church or of the evening sacrifice of the next day, the sacrifice, that is, which, raising his hands, he offered to the Father at the end of the ages for the salvation of the whole world."[7] Again, in order to fix our hope on the light that knows no setting, "we pray and make petition for the light to come down on us anew; we implore the coming of Christ who will bring the grace of eternal light."[8] Finally, at this hour we join with the Churches of the East in calling upon the "joy-giving light of that holy glory, born of the immortal, heavenly Father, the holy and blessed Jesus Christ; now that we have come to the setting of the sun and have seen the evening star, we sing in praise of God, Father, Son, and Holy Spirit . . . ."

40.   Morning prayer and evening prayer are therefore to be accorded the highest importance as the prayer of the Christian community. Their public or communal celebration should be encouraged, especially in the case of those who live in community. Indeed, the recitation of these hours should be recommended also to individual members of the faithful unable to take part in a celebration in common.

41.   Morning prayer and evening prayer begin with the introductory verse, *God, come to my assistance. Lord, make haste to help me.* There follows the *Glory to the Father*, with *As it was in the beginning* and *Alleluia* (omitted in Lent). This introduction is omitted at morning prayer when the invitatory immediately precedes it.

42.   Then an appropriate hymn is sung immediately. The purpose of the hymn is to set the tone for the hour or the feast and, especially in celebrations with a congregation, to form a simple and pleasant introduction to prayer.

43.   After the hymn the psalmody follows, in accordance with the rules laid down in nos. 121–125. The psalmody of morning prayer consists of one morning psalm, then a canticle from the Old Testament and, finally, a second psalm of praise, following the tradition of the Church.

   The psalmody of evening prayer consists of two psalms (or two parts of a longer psalm) suited to the hour and to celebration with a congregation and a canticle from the letters of the apostles or from the Book of Revelation.

44.   After the psalmody there is either a short reading or a longer one.

45.   The short reading is provided to fit the day, the season, and the feast. It is to be read and received as a true proclamation of God's word that emphasizes some holy thought or highlights some shorter passages that may be overlooked in the continuous cycle of Scripture readings.

   The short readings are different for each day of the psalter cycle.

46.   Especially in a celebration with a congregation, a longer Scripture reading may be chosen either from the office of readings or the Lectionary for Mass, particularly texts that for some reason have not been used. From time to time some other more suitable reading may be used, in accordance with the rules in nos. 248–249 and 251.

47.   In a celebration with a congregation a short homily may follow the reading to explain its meaning, as circumstances suggest.

48.   After the reading or homily a period of silence may be observed.

49.   As a response to the word of God, a responsorial chant or short responsory is provided; this may be omitted. Other chants with the same

purpose and character may also be substituted in its place, provided these have been duly approved by the conference of bishops.

50.   Next is the solemn recitation of the gospel canticle with its antiphon, that is, the Canticle of Zechariah at morning prayer and the Canticle of Mary at evening prayer. Sanctioned by age-old popular usage in the Roman Church, these canticles are expressions of praise and thanksgiving for our redemption. The antiphon for each canticle is indicated, according to the character of the day, the season, or the feast.

51.   After the canticle, at morning prayer come the petitions for the consecration of the day and its work to God and at evening prayer, the intercessions (see nos. 179–193).

52.   After the petitions or intercessions the Lord's Prayer is said by all.

53.   Immediately after the Lord's Prayer there follows the concluding prayer, which for weekdays in Ordinary Time is found in the psalter and for other days in the proper.

54.   Then, if a priest or deacon is presiding, he dismisses the congregation with the greeting, *The Lord be with you,* and the blessing as at Mass. He adds the invitation, *Go in peace. R. Thanks be to God.* In the absence of a priest or deacon the celebration concludes with *May the Lord bless us,* etc.

III. OFFICE OF READINGS

55.   The office of readings seeks to provide God's people, and in particular those consecrated to God in a special way, with a wider selection of passages from sacred Scripture for meditation, together with the finest excerpts from spiritual writers. Even though the cycle of scriptural readings at daily Mass is now richer, the treasures of revelation and tradition to be found in the office of readings will also contribute greatly to the spiritual life. Bishops and priests in particular should prize these treasures, so that they may hand on to others the word of God they have themselves received and make their teaching "the true nourishment for the people of God."[9]

56.   But prayer should accompany "the reading of sacred Scripture so that there may be a conversation between God and his people: 'we talk

with God when we pray, we listen to him when we read God's words.' "[10]
For this reason the office of readings consists also of psalms, a hymn, a
prayer, and other texts, giving it the character of true prayer.

57.   The Constitution on the Liturgy directs that the office of readings,
"though it should retain its character as a night office of praise when celebrated in choir, shall be adapted so that it may be recited at any hour of
the day; it shall be made up of fewer psalms and longer readings."[11]

58.   Those who are obliged by their own particular law and others who
commendably wish to retain the character of this office as a night office
of praise (either by saying it at night or very early in the morning and
before morning prayer), during Ordinary Time choose the hymn from the
selection given for this purpose. Moreover, for Sundays, solemnities, and
certain feasts what is said in nos. 70–73 about vigils must be kept in mind.

59.   Without prejudice to the regulations just given, the office of readings may be recited at any hour of the day, even during the night hours
of the previous day, after evening prayer has been said.

60.   If the office of readings is said before morning prayer, the invitatory precedes it, as noted (nos. 34–36). Otherwise it begins with the
verse, *God, come to my assistance* with the *Glory to the Father, As it was
in the beginning*, and the *Alleluia* (omitted in Lent).

61.   Then the hymn is sung. In Ordinary Time this is taken either from
the night selections, as already indicated (nos. 34–36), or from the morning selections, depending on what the true time of day requires.

62.   The psalmody follows and consists of three psalms (or parts in the
case of longer psalms). During the Easter triduum, on days within the octaves of Easter and Christmas, on solemnities and feasts, the psalms are
proper, with their proper antiphons.
        On Sundays and weekdays, however, the psalms and their antiphons
are taken from the current week and day of the psalter. On memorials of
the saints they are similarly taken from the current week and day of the
psalter, unless there are proper psalms or antiphons (see nos. 218ff.).

63.   Between the psalmody and the readings there is, as a rule, a verse,
marking a transition in the prayer from psalmody to listening.

64.   There are two readings: the first is from the Scriptures, the second is from the writings of the Fathers or church writers, or else is a reading connected with the saints.

65.   After each reading there is a responsory (see nos. 169–172).

66.   The scriptural reading is normally to be taken from the Proper of Seasons, in accordance with the rules to be given later (nos. 140–155). On solemnities and feasts, however, it is taken from the proper or the common.

67.   On solemnities and feasts of saints a proper second reading is used; if there is none, the second reading is taken from the respective Common of Saints. On memorials of saints when the celebration is not impeded, the reading in connection with the saint replaces the current second reading (see nos. 166 and 235).

68.   On Sundays outside Lent, on days within the octaves of Easter and Christmas, and on solemnities and feasts the *Te Deum* is said after the second reading with its responsory but is omitted on memorials and weekdays. The last part of this hymn, that is, from the verse, *Save your people, Lord* to the end, may be omitted.

69.   The office of readings normally concludes with the prayer proper to the day and, at least in recitation in common, with the acclamation, *Let us praise the Lord. R. And give him thanks.*

IV. VIGILS

70.   The Easter Vigil is celebrated by the whole Church, in the rites given in the relevant liturgical books. "The vigil of this night," as St. Augustine said, "is of such importance that it could claim exclusively for itself the name 'vigil,' common though this is to all the others."[12] "We keep vigil on that night when the Lord rose again and inaugurated for us in his humanity that life . . . in which there is neither death nor sleep. . . . Hence, the one whose resurrection we celebrate by keeping watch a little longer will see to it that we reign with him by living a life without end."[13]

71.   As with the Easter Vigil, it was customary to begin certain solemnities (different in different Churches) with a vigil. Among these solemnities Christmas and Pentecost are preeminent. This custom should be

maintained and fostered, according to the particular usage of each Church. Whenever it seems good to add a vigil for other solemnities or pilgrimages, the general norms for celebrations of the word should be followed.

72.   The Fathers and spiritual writers have frequently encouraged Christians, especially those who lead the contemplative life, to pray during the night. Such prayer expresses and awakens our expectation of the Lord's Second Coming: "At midnight the cry went up: 'See, the bridegroom is coming, go out to meet him' " (Mt 25:6). "Keep watch, then, for you do not know when the master of the house is coming, whether late or at midnight or at cockcrow or in the morning, so that if he comes unexpectedly he may not find you sleeping" (Mk 13:35–36). All who maintain the character of the office of readings as a night office, therefore, are to be commended.

73.   Further, since in the Roman Rite the office of readings is always of a uniform brevity, especially for the sake of those engaged in apostolic work, those who desire, in accordance with tradition, to extend the celebration of the vigils of Sundays, solemnities, and feasts should do so as follows.

First, the office of readings is to be celebrated as in *The Liturgy of the Hours* up to the end of the readings. After the two readings and before the *Te Deum* canticles should be added from the special appendix of *The Liturgy of the Hours*. Then the gospel should be read; a homily on the gospel may be added. After this the *Te Deum* is sung and the prayer said.

On solemnities and feasts the gospel is to be taken from the Lectionary for Mass; on Sundays, from the series on the paschal mystery in the appendix of *The Liturgy of the Hours*.

V. DAYTIME HOURS

74.   Following a very ancient tradition Christians have made a practice of praying out of private devotion at various times of the day, even in the course of their work, in imitation of the Church in apostolic times. In different ways with the passage of time this tradition has taken the form of a liturgical celebration.

75.   Liturgical custom in both East and West has retained midmorning, midday, and midafternoon prayer, mainly because these hours were

linked to a commemoration of the events of the Lord's passion and of the first preaching of the Gospel.

76.   Vatican Council II decreed that these lesser hours are to be retained in choir.[14]

The liturgical practice of saying these three hours is to be retained, without prejudice to particular law, by those who live the contemplative life. It is recommended also for all, especially those who take part in retreats or pastoral meetings.

77.   Outside choir, without prejudice to particular law, it is permitted to choose from the three hours the one most appropriate to the time of day, so that the tradition of prayer in the course of the day's work may be maintained.

78.   Daytime prayer is so arranged as to take into account both those who recite only one hour and those who are obliged, or desire, to say all three hours.

79.   The daytime hours begin with the introductory verse, *God, come to my assistance* with the *Glory to the Father, As it was in the beginning*, and the *Alleluia* (omitted in Lent). Then a hymn appropriate to the hour is sung. The psalmody is next, then the reading, followed by the verse. The hour concludes with the prayer and, at least in recitation in common, with the acclamation, *Let us praise the Lord. R. And give him thanks.*

80.   Different hymns and prayers are given for each of the hours so that, in keeping with tradition, they may correspond to the true time of day and thus sanctify it in a more pointed way. Those who recite only one hour should therefore choose the texts that correspond to the true time of day.

In addition, the readings and prayers vary in keeping with the character of the day, the season, or the feast.

81.   Two psalmodies are provided; the current psalmody and the complementary psalmody. Those who pray one hour should use the current psalmody. Those who pray more than one hour should use the current psalmody at one hour and the complementary psalmody at the others.

82.   The current psalmody consists of three psalms (or parts in the case of longer psalms) from the psalter, with their antiphons, unless directions are given to the contrary.

On solemnities, the Easter triduum, and days within the octave of Easter, proper antiphons are said with three psalms chosen from the complementary psalmody, unless special psalms are to be used or the celebration falls on a Sunday, when the psalms are those from the Sunday of Week I of the psalter.

83.   The complementary psalter consists of three sets of three psalms, chosen as a rule from the Gradual Psalms.

VI. NIGHT PRAYER

84.   Night prayer is the last prayer of the day, said before retiring, even if that is after midnight.

85.   Night prayer begins like the other hours, with the verse, *God, come to my assistance*, the *Glory to the Father, As it was in the beginning*, and the *Alleluia* (omitted in Lent).

86.   It is a laudable practice to have next an examination of conscience; in a celebration in common this takes place in silence or as part of a penitential rite based on the formularies in the Roman Missal.

87.   The appropriate hymn follows.

88.   After evening prayer I of Sunday the psalmody consists of Ps 4 and Ps 134; after evening prayer II of Sunday it consists of Ps 91.

On the other days psalms are chosen that are full of confidence in the Lord; it is permissible to use the Sunday psalms instead, especially for the convenience of those who may wish to pray night prayer from memory.

89.   After the psalmody there is a reading, followed by the responsory, *Into your hands*. Then, as a climax to the whole hour, the Canticle of Simeon, *Lord, now you let your servant go in peace* follows, with its antiphon.

90.   The concluding prayer then follows, as it appears in the psalter.

91.   After the prayer the blessing, *May the all-powerful Lord* is used, even in private recitation.

92.   Finally, one of the antiphons in honor of the Blessed Virgin Mary is said. In the Easter season this is always to be the *Regina caeli*. In addition to the antiphons given in *The Liturgy of the Hours*, others may be approved by the conferences of bishops. [15]

VII. COMBINING THE HOURS WITH MASS OR WITH EACH OTHER

93.   In particular cases, if circumstances require, it is possible to link an hour more closely with Mass when there is a celebration of the liturgy of the hours in public or in common, according to the norms that follow, provided the Mass and the hour belong to one and the same office. Care must be taken, however, that this does not result in harm to pastoral work, especially on Sundays.

94.   When morning prayer, celebrated in choir or in common, comes immediately before Mass, the whole celebration may begin either with the introductory verse and hymn of morning prayer, especially on weekdays, or with the entrance song, procession, and celebrant's greeting, especially on Sundays and holydays; one of the introductory rites is thus omitted.

The psalmody of morning prayer follows as usual, up to, but excluding, the reading. After the psalmody the penitential rite is omitted and, as circumstances suggest, the *Kyrie*; the *Gloria* then follows, if required by the rubrics, and the celebrant says the opening prayer of the Mass. The liturgy of the word follows as usual.

The general intercessions are made in the place and form customary at Mass. But on weekdays, at Mass in the morning, the intercessions of morning prayer may replace the daily form of the general intercessions at Mass.

After the communion with its communion song the Canticle of Zechariah, *Blessed be the Lord*, with its antiphon from morning prayer, is sung. Then follow the prayer after communion and the rest as usual.

95.   If public celebration of a daytime hour, whichever corresponds to the time of day, is immediately followed by Mass, the whole celebration may begin in the same way, either with the introductory verse and hymn for the hour, especially on weekdays, or with the entrance song, proces-

sion, and celebrant's greeting, especially on Sundays and holydays; one of the introductory rites is thus omitted.

The psalmody of the hour follows as usual up to, but excluding, the reading. After the psalmody the penitential rite is omitted and, as circumstances suggest, the *Kyrie*; the *Gloria* then follows, if required by the rubrics and the celebrant says the opening prayer of the Mass.

96.   Evening prayer, celebrated immediately before Mass, is joined to it in the same way as morning prayer. Evening prayer I of solemnities, Sundays, or feasts of the Lord falling on Sundays may not be celebrated until after Mass of the preceding day or Saturday.

97.   When a daytime hour or evening prayer follows Mass, the Mass is celebrated in the usual way up to and including the prayer after communion.

When the prayer after communion has been said, the psalmody of the hour begins without introduction. At the daytime hour, after the psalmody the short reading is omitted and the prayer is said at once and the dismissal takes place as at Mass. At evening prayer, after the psalmody the short reading is omitted and the Canticle of Mary with its antiphon follows at once; the intercessions and the Lord's Prayer are omitted; the concluding prayer follows, then the blessing of the congregation.

98.   Apart from Christmas eve, the combining of Mass with the office of readings is normally excluded, since the Mass already has its own cycle of readings, to be kept distinct from any other. But if by way of exception, it should be necessary to join the two, then immediately after the second reading from the office, with its responsory, the rest is omitted and the Mass begins with the *Gloria*, if it is called for; otherwise the Mass begins with the opening prayer.

99.   If the office of readings comes immediately before another hour of the office, then the appropriate hymn for that hour may be sung at the beginning of the office of readings. At the end of the office of readings the prayer and conclusion are omitted and in the hour following the introductory verse with the *Glory to the Father* is omitted.

◇ *Chapter III*

Different Elements in The Liturgy of the Hours

I. PSALMS AND THEIR CONNECTION WITH CHRISTIAN PRAYER

100.   In the liturgy of the hours the Church in large measure prays through the magnificent songs that the Old Testament authors composed under the inspiration of the Holy Spirit. The origin of these verses gives them great power to raise the mind to God, to inspire devotion, to evoke gratitude in times of favor, and to bring consolation and courage in times of trial.

101.   The psalms, however, are only a foreshadowing of the fullness of time that came to pass in Christ the Lord and that is the source of the power of the Church's prayer. Hence, while the Christian people are all agreed on the supreme value to be placed on the psalms, they can sometimes experience difficulty in making this inspired poetry their own prayer.

102.   Yet the Holy Spirit, under whose inspiration the psalms were written, is always present by his grace to those believers who use them with good will. But more is necessary: the faithful must "improve their understanding of the Bible, especially of the psalms,"[1] according to their individual capacity, so that they may understand how and by what method they can truly pray through the psalms.

103.   The psalms are not readings or prose prayers, but poems of praise. They can on occasion be recited as readings, but from their literary genre they are properly called *Tehillim* ("songs of praise") in Hebrew and *psalmoi* ("songs to be sung to the lyre") in Greek. In fact, all the psalms have a musical quality that determines their correct style of delivery. Thus even when a psalm is recited and not sung or is said silently in private, its musical character should govern its use. A psalm does present a text to

the minds of the people, but its aim is to move the heart of those singing it or listening to it and also of those accompanying it "on the lyre and harp."

104.   To sing the psalms with understanding, then, is to meditate on them verse by verse, with the heart always ready to respond in the way the Holy Spirit desires. The one who inspired the psalmist will also be present to those who in faith and love are ready to receive his grace. For this reason the singing of psalms, though it demands the reverence owed to God's majesty, should be the expression of a joyful spirit and a loving heart, in keeping with their character as sacred poetry and divine song and above all with the freedom of the children of God.

105.   Often the words of a psalm help us to pray with greater ease and fervor, whether in thanksgiving and joyful praise of God or in prayer for help in the throes of suffering. But difficulties may arise, especially when the psalm is not addressed directly to God. The psalmist is a poet and often addresses the people as he recalls Israel's history; sometimes he addresses others, including subrational creatures. He even represents the words as being spoken by God himself and individual people, including, as in Ps 2, God's enemies. This shows that a psalm is a different kind of prayer from a prayer or collect composed by the Church. Moreover, it is in keeping with the poetic and musical character of the psalms that they do not necessarily address God but are sung in God's presence. Thus St. Benedict's instruction: "Let us reflect on what it means to be in the sight of God and his angels, and let us so stand in his presence that our minds are in harmony with our voices."[2]

106.   In praying the psalms we should open our hearts to the different attitudes they express, varying with the literary genre to which each belongs (psalms of grief, trust, gratitude, etc.) and to which biblical scholars rightly attach great importance.

107.   Staying close to the meaning of the words, the person who prays the psalms looks for the significance of the text for the human life of the believer.
    It is clear that each psalm was written in its own individual circumstances, which the titles given for each psalm in the Hebrew psalter are meant to indicate. But whatever its historical origin, each psalm has its own meaning, which we cannot overlook even in our own day. Though the psalms originated very many centuries ago among an Eastern people,

they express accurately the pain and hope, the unhappiness and trust of people of every age and country, and sing above all of faith in God, of revelation, and of redemption.

108. Those who pray the psalms in the liturgy of the hours do so not so much in their own name as in the name of the entire Body of Christ. This consideration does away with the problem of a possible discrepancy between personal feelings and the sentiments a psalm is expressing: for example, when a person feels sad and the psalm is one of joy or when a person feels happy and the psalm is one of mourning. Such a problem is readily solved in private prayer, which allows for the choice of a psalm suited to personal feelings. The divine office, however, is not private; the cycle of psalms is public, in the name of the Church, even for those who may be reciting an hour alone. Those who pray the psalms in the name of the Church nevertheless can always find a reason for joy or sadness, for the saying of the Apostle applies in this case also: "Rejoice with the joyful and weep with those who weep" (Rom 12:15). In this way human frailty, wounded by self-love, is healed in proportion to the love that makes the heart match the voice that prays the psalms.[3]

109. Those who pray the psalms in the name of the Church should be aware of their full sense (*sensus plenus*), especially their Messianic sense, which was the reason for the Church's introduction of the psalter into its prayer. This Messianic sense was fully revealed in the New Testament and indeed was affirmed publicly by Christ the Lord in person when he said to the apostles: "All that is written about me in the law of Moses and the prophets and the psalms must be fulfilled" (Lk 24:44). The best-known example of this Messianic sense is the dialogue in Matthew's Gospel on the Messiah as Son of David and David's Lord,[4] where Ps 110 is interpreted as Messianic.

Following this line of thought, the Fathers of the Church saw the whole psalter as a prophecy of Christ and the Church and explained it in this sense; for the same reason the psalms have been chosen for use in the liturgy. Though somewhat contrived interpretations were at times proposed, in general the Fathers and the liturgy itself had the right to hear in the singing of the psalms the voice of Christ crying out to the Father or of the Father conversing with the Son; indeed, they also recognized in the psalms the voice of the Church, the apostles, and the martyrs. This method of interpretation also flourished in the Middle Ages; in many manuscripts of the period the Christological meaning of each psalm was set before those praying by means of the caption prefixed. A Christological meaning is by no means confined to the recognized Messianic psalms but is given also to many others. Some of these interpretations are doubtless Christological only in an accommodated sense, but they have the support of the Church's tradition.

On the great feasts especially, the choice of psalms is often based on their Christological meaning and antiphons taken from these psalms are frequently used to throw light on this meaning.

II. ANTIPHONS AND OTHER AIDS TO PRAYING THE PSALMS

110.   In the Latin tradition of psalmody three elements have greatly contributed to an understanding of the psalms and their use as Christian prayer: the captions, the psalm-prayers, and in particular the antiphons.

111.   In the psalter of *The Liturgy of the Hours* a caption is given for each psalm to explain its meaning and its import for the personal life of the believer. These captions are intended only as an aid to prayer. A quotation from the New Testament or the Fathers of the Church is added to foster prayer in the light of Christ's new revelation; it is an invitation to pray the psalms in their Christological meaning.

112.   Psalm-prayers for each psalm are given in the supplement to *The Liturgy of the Hours* as an aid to understanding them in a predominantly Christian way. An ancient tradition provides a model for their use: after the psalm a period of silence is observed, then the prayer gives a resumé and resolution of the thoughts and aspirations of those praying the psalms.

113.   Even when the liturgy of the hours is recited, not sung, each psalm retains its own antiphon, which is also to be said in private recitation. The antiphons help to bring out the literary genre of the psalm; they highlight some theme that may otherwise not attract the attention it deserves; they suggest an individual tone in a psalm, varying with different contexts: indeed, as long as farfetched accommodated senses are avoided, antiphons are of great value in helping toward an understanding of the typological meaning or the meaning appropriate to the feast; they can also add pleasure and variety to the recitation of the psalms.

114.   The antiphons in the psalter have been designed to lend themselves to vernacular translation and to repetition after each strophe, in

accordance with no. 125. When the office of Ordinary Time is recited, not sung, the quotations printed with the psalms may be used in place of these antiphons (see no. 111).

115.   When a psalm may be divided because of its length into several sections within one and the same hour, an antiphon is given for each section. This is to provide variety, especially when the hour is sung, and also to help toward a better understanding of the riches of the psalm. Still, it is permissible to say or sing the complete psalm without interruption, using only the first antiphon.

116.   Proper antiphons are given for each of the psalms of morning prayer and evening prayer during the Easter triduum, on the days within the octaves of Easter and Christmas, on the Sundays of the seasons of Advent, Christmas, Lent, and Easter, on the weekdays of Holy Week and the Easter season, and from the 17th to the 24th of December.

117.   On solemnities proper antiphons are given for the office of readings, morning prayer, the daytime hours, and evening prayer; if not, the antiphons are taken from the common. On feasts the same applies to the office of readings and to morning prayer and evening prayer.

118.   Any memorials of the saints that have proper antiphons retain them (see no. 235).

119.   The antiphons for the Canticles of Zechariah and of Mary are taken, during Ordinary Time, from the Proper of Seasons, if they are given there; if not, they are taken from the current week and day of the psalter. On solemnities and feasts they are taken from the proper if they are given there; if not, they are taken from the common. On memorials without proper antiphons the antiphon may be taken at will either from the common or from the current week.

120.   During the Easter season *Alleluia* is added to all antiphons, unless it would clash with the meaning of a particular antiphon.

III. WAYS OF SINGING THE PSALMS

121.   Different psalms may be sung in different ways for a fuller grasp of their spiritual meaning and beauty. The choice of ways is dictated by the literary genre or length of each psalm, by the language used, whether

Latin or the vernacular, and especially by the kind of celebration, whether individual, with a group, or with a congregation. The reason for using psalms is not the establishment of a fixed amount of prayer but their own variety and the character proper to each.

122.   The psalms are sung or said in one of three ways, according to the different usages established in tradition or experience: directly (*in directum*), that is, all sing the entire psalm, or antiphonally, that is, two choirs or sections of the congregation sing alternate verses or strophes, or responsorially.

123.   At the beginning of each psalm its own antiphon is always to be recited, as noted in nos. 113–120. At the end of the psalm the practice of concluding with the *Glory to the Father* and *As it was in the beginning* is retained. This is the fitting conclusion endorsed by tradition and it gives to Old Testament prayer a note of praise and a Christological and Trinitarian sense. The antiphon may be repeated at the end of the psalm.

124.   When longer psalms occur, sections are marked in the psalter that divide the parts in such a way as to keep the threefold structure of the hour; but great care has been taken not to distort the meaning of the psalm.

It is useful to observe this division, especially in a choral celebration in Latin; the *Glory to the Father* is added at the end of each section.

It is permissible, however, either to keep this traditional way or to pause between the different sections of the same psalm or to recite the whole psalm and its antiphon as a single unit without a break.

125.   In addition, when the literary genre of a psalm suggests it, the divisions into strophes are marked in order that, especially when the psalm is sung in the vernacular, the antiphons may be repeated after each strophe; in this case the *Glory to the Father* need be said only at the end of the psalm.

IV. PLAN FOR THE DISTRIBUTION OF THE PSALMS IN THE OFFICE

126.   The psalms are distributed over a four-week cycle in such a way that very few psalms are omitted, while some, traditionally more important, occur more frequently than others; morning prayer and evening

prayer as well as night prayer have been assigned to psalms appropriate to these hours.[5]

127.   Since morning prayer and evening prayer are particularly designed for celebration with a congregation, the psalms chosen for them are those more suited to this purpose.

128.   For night prayer the norm given in no. 88 has been followed.

129.   For Sunday, including its office of readings and daytime prayer, the psalms chosen are those that tradition has particularly singled out as expressions of the paschal mystery. Certain psalms of a penitential character or connected with the passion are assigned to Friday.

130.   Three psalms (78, 105, and 106) are reserved for the seasons of Advent, Christmas, Lent, and Easter, because they throw a special light on the Old Testament history of salvation as the forerunner of its fulfillment in the New.

131.   Three psalms (58, 83, and 109) have been omitted from the psalter cycle because of their curses; in the same way, some verses have been omitted from certain psalms, as noted at the head of each. The reason for the omission is a certain psychological difficulty, even though the psalms of imprecation are in fact used as prayer in the New Testament, for example, Rv 6:10, and in no sense to encourage the use of curses.

132.   Psalms too long to be included in one hour of the office are assigned to the same hour on different days so that they may be recited in full by those who do not usually say other hours. Thus Ps 119 is divided in keeping with its own internal structure and is spread over twenty-two days during daytime prayer, because tradition has assigned it to the day hours.

133.   The four-week cycle of the psalter is coordinated with the liturgical year in such a way that on the First Sunday of Advent, the First Sunday in Ordinary Time, the First Sunday of Lent, and Easter Sunday the cycle is always begun again with Week I (others being omitted when necessary).

After Pentecost, when the psalter cycle follows the series of weeks in Ordinary Time, it begins with the week indicated in the Proper of Seasons at the beginning of the appropriate week in Ordinary Time.

134.   On solemnities and feasts, during the Easter triduum, and on the days within the octaves of Easter and Christmas, proper psalms are assigned to the office of readings from those with a tradition of use at these times and their relevance is generally highlighted by the choice of antiphon. This is also the case at daytime prayer on certain solemnities of the Lord and during the octave of Easter. At morning prayer the psalms and canticle are taken from the Sunday of the Week I of the psalter. On solemnities the psalms at evening prayer I are taken from the *Laudate* Psalms, following an ancient custom. At evening prayer II on solemnities and at evening prayer on feasts the psalms and canticle are proper. At daytime prayer on solemnities (except those already mentioned and those falling on Sunday) the psalms are taken from the Gradual Psalms; at daytime prayer on feasts the psalms are those of the current week and day of the psalter.

135.   In all other cases the psalms are taken from the current week and day of the psalter, unless there are proper antiphons or proper psalms.

V. CANTICLES FROM THE OLD AND NEW TESTAMENTS

136.   At morning prayer between the first and the second psalm a canticle from the Old Testament is inserted, in accordance with custom. In addition to the series handed down from the ancient Roman tradition and the other series introduced into the breviary by St. Pius X, several other canticles have been added to the psalter from different books of the Old Testament, in order that each weekday of the four-week cycle may have its own proper canticle and on Sunday the two sections of the Canticle of the Three Children may be alternated.

137.   At evening prayer, after the two psalms, a canticle of the New Testament is inserted, from the letters of the apostles or the Book of Revelation. Seven canticles are given for each week of the four-week cycle, one for each day. On the Sundays of Lent, however, in place of the *Alleluia* Canticle from the Book of Revelation, the canticle is from the First Letter of Peter. In addition, on the solemnity of the Epiphany and the feast of the Transfiguration the canticle is from the First Letter to Timothy; this is indicated in those offices.

138.   The gospel Canticles of Zechariah, of Mary, and of Simeon are to be treated with the same solemnity and dignity as are customary at the proclamation of the gospel itself.

139.   Both psalmody and readings are arranged in keeping with the received rule of tradition that the Old Testament is read first, then the writings of the apostles, and finally the gospel.

VI. READINGS FROM SACRED SCRIPTURE

A. Reading of Sacred Scripture in General

140.   The reading of sacred Scripture, which, following an ancient tradition, takes place publicly in the liturgy, is to have special importance for all Christians, not only in the celebration of the eucharist but also in the divine office. The reason is that this reading is not the result of individual choice or devotion but is the planned decision of the Church itself, in order that in the course of the year the Bride of Christ may unfold the mystery of Christ "from his incarnation and birth until his ascension, the day of Pentecost, and the expectation of blessed hope and of the Lord's return."[6] In addition, the reading of sacred Scripture in the liturgical celebration is always accompanied by prayer in order that the reading may have greater effect and that, in turn, prayer—especially the praying of the psalms—may gain fuller understanding and become more fervent and devout because of the reading.

141.   In the liturgy of the hours there is a longer reading of sacred Scripture and a shorter reading.

142.   The longer reading, optional at morning prayer and evening prayer, is described in no. 46.

B. Cycle of Scripture Readings in the Office of Readings

143.   The cycle of readings from sacred Scripture in the office of readings takes into account both those special seasons during which by an ancient tradition particular books are to be read and the cycle of readings at Mass. The liturgy of the hours is thus coordinated with the Mass in such a way that the scriptural readings in the office complement the readings at Mass and so provide a complete view of the history of salvation.

144.   Without prejudice to the exception noted in no. 73, there are no readings from the Gospel in the liturgy of the hours, since in the Mass each year the Gospel is read in its entirety.

145.   There are two cycles of biblical readings. The first is a one-year cycle and is incorporated into *The Liturgy of the Hours*; the second, given in the supplement for optional use, is a two-year cycle, like the cycle of readings at weekday Masses in Ordinary Time.

146.   The two-year cycle of readings for the liturgy of the hours is so arranged that each year there are readings from nearly all the books of sacred Scripture as well as longer and more difficult texts that are not suitable for inclusion in the Mass. The New Testament as a whole is read each year, partly in the Mass, partly in the liturgy of the hours; but for the Old Testament books a selection has been made of those parts that are of greater importance for the understanding of the history of salvation and for deepening devotion.

The complementarity between the readings in the liturgy of the hours and in the Mass in no way assigns the same texts to the same days or spreads the same books over the same seasons. This would leave the liturgy of the hours with the less important passages and upset the sequence of texts. Rather this complementarity necessarily demands that the same book be used in the Mass and in the liturgy of the hours in alternate years or that, if it is read in the same year, there be some interval in between.

147.   During Advent, following an ancient tradition, passages are read from Isaiah in a semicontinuous sequence, alternating in a two-year cycle. In addition, the Book of Ruth and certain prophecies from Micah are read. Since there are special readings from 17 to 24 December (both dates included), readings for the Third Week of Advent which fall on these dates are omitted.

148.   From 29 December until 5 January the readings for Year I are taken from the Letter to the Colossians (which considers the incarnation of the Lord within the context of the whole history of salvation) and the readings for Year II are taken from the Song of Songs (which foreshadows the union of God and humanity in Christ): "God the Father prepared a wedding feast for God his Son when he united him with human nature in the womb of the Virgin, when he who is God before all ages willed that his Son should become man at the end of the ages."[7]

149.   From 7 January until the Saturday after the Epiphany the readings are eschatological texts from Isaiah 60–66 and Baruch. Readings remaining unused are omitted for that year.

150.   During Lent the readings for the first year are passages from Deuteronomy and the Letter to the Hebrews. Those for the second year review the history of salvation from Exodus, Leviticus, and Numbers. The Letter to the Hebrews interprets the Old Covenant in the light of the paschal mystery of Christ. A passage from the same letter, on Christ's sacrifice (Heb 9:11–28), is read on Good Friday; another, on the Lord's rest (Heb 4:1–16), is read on Holy Saturday. On the other days of Holy Week the readings in Year I are the third and fourth Songs of the Servant of the Lord and extracts from Lamentations; in Year II the prophet Jeremiah is read, as a type of Christ in his passion.

151.   During the Easter season, apart from the First and Second Sundays of Easter and the solemnities of the Ascension and Pentecost, there are the traditional readings from the First Letter of Peter, the Book of Revelation, and the Letters of John (for Year I), and from the Acts of the Apostles (for Year II).

152.   From the Monday after the feast of the Baptism of the Lord until Lent and from the Monday after Pentecost until Advent there is a continuous series of thirty-four weeks in Ordinary Time.

This series is interrupted from Ash Wednesday until Pentecost. On the Monday after Pentecost Sunday the cycle of readings in Ordinary Time is resumed, beginning with the week after the one interrupted because of Lent; the reading assigned to the Sunday is omitted.

In years with only thirty-three weeks in Ordinary Time, the week immediately following Pentecost is dropped, in order to retain the readings of the last weeks, which are eschatological readings.

The books of the Old Testament are arranged so as to follow the history of salvation: God reveals himself in the history of his people as he leads and enlightens them in progressive stages. This is why prophetic books are read along with the historical books, but with due consideration of the period in which the prophets lived and taught. Hence, the cycle of readings from the Old Testament contains, in Year I, the historical books and prophetic utterances from the Book of Joshua as far as, and including, the time of the exile. In Year II, after the readings from Genesis (read before Lent), the history of salvation is resumed after the exile up to the time of the Maccabees. Year II includes the later prophets, the wisdom literature, and the narratives in Esther, Tobit, and Judith.

The letters of the apostles not read at special times are distributed through the year in a way that takes into account the readings at Mass and the chronological order in which these letters were written.

153.   The one-year cycle is shortened in such a way that each year special passages from sacred Scripture are read, but in correlation with the two-year cycle of readings at Mass, to which it is intended to be complementary.

154.   Proper readings are assigned for solemnities and feasts; otherwise the readings are taken from the respective Common of Saints.

155.   As far as possible, each passage read keeps to a certain unity. In order therefore to strike a balance in length (otherwise difficult to achieve in view of the different literary genres of the books), some verses are occasionally omitted, though omissions are always noted. But it is permissible and commendable to read the complete passage from an approved text.

C. Short Readings

156.   The short readings or "chapters" (*capitula*) are referred to in no. 45, which describes their importance in the liturgy of the hours. They have been chosen to give clear and concise expression to a theme or an exhortation. Care has also been taken to ensure variety.

157.   Accordingly, four weekly series of short readings have been composed for Ordinary Time. They are incorporated into the psalter in such a way that the reading changes during the four weeks. There are also weekly series for the seasons of Advent, Christmas, Lent, and Easter. In addition there are proper short readings for solemnities, feasts, and some memorials, as well as a one-week series for night prayer.

158.   The following determined the choice of short readings:
a. in accordance with tradition, exclusion of the Gospels;
b. respect for the special character of Sunday, or even of Friday, and of the individual hours;
c. use only of the New Testament for the readings at evening prayer, following as they do a New Testament canticle.

VII. READINGS FROM THE FATHERS AND CHURCH WRITERS

159.   In keeping with the tradition of the Roman Church the office of readings has, after the biblical reading, a reading from the Fathers or

church writers, with a responsory, unless there is to be a reading relating to a saint (see nos. 228–239).

160.   Texts for this reading are given from the writings of the Fathers and doctors of the Church and from other ecclesiastical writers of the Eastern and Western Church. Pride of place is given to the Fathers because of their distinctive authority in the Church.

161.   In addition to the readings that *The Liturgy of the Hours* assigns to each day, the optional lectionary supplies a larger collection, in order that the treasures of the Church's tradition may be more widely available to those who pray the liturgy of the hours. Everyone is free to take the second reading either from *The Liturgy of the Hours* or from the optional lectionary.

162.   Further, the conferences of bishops may prepare additional texts, adapted to the traditions and culture of their own region,[8] for inclusion in the optional lectionary as a supplement. These texts are to be taken from the works of Catholic writers, outstanding for their teaching and holiness of life.

163.   The purpose of the second reading is principally to provide for meditation on the word of God as received by the Church in its tradition. The Church has always been convinced of the need to teach the word of God authentically to believers, so that "the line of interpretation regarding the prophets and apostles may be guided by an ecclesial and catholic understanding."[9]

164.   By constant use of the writings handed down by the universal tradition of the Church, those who read them are led to a deeper reflection on sacred Scripture and to a relish and love for it. The writings of the Fathers are an outstanding witness to the contemplation of the word of God over the centuries by the Bride of the incarnate Word: the Church, "possessing the counsel and spirit of its Bridegroom and God,"[10] is always seeking to attain a more profound understanding of the sacred Scriptures.

165.   The reading of the Fathers leads Christians to an understanding also of the liturgical seasons and feasts. In addition, it gives them access

to the priceless spiritual treasures that form the unique patrimony of the Church and provide a firm foundation for the spiritual life and a rich source for increasing devotion. Preachers of God's word also have at hand each day superb examples of sacred preaching.

VIII. READINGS IN HONOR OF SAINTS

166. The "hagiographical" readings or readings in honor of saints are either texts from a Father of the Church or another ecclesiastical writer, referring specifically or rightly applicable to the saint being commemorated, or the readings are texts from the saint's own writings, or are biographical.

167. Those who compose particular propers for saints must ensure historical accuracy[11] as well as genuine spiritual benefit for those who will read or hear the readings about the saints. Anything that merely excites amazement should be carefully avoided. Emphasis should be given to the individual spiritual characteristics of the saints, in a way suited to modern conditions; stress should also be laid on their contribution to the life and spirituality of the Church.

168. A short biographical note, simply giving historical facts and a brief sketch of the saint's life, is provided at the head of the reading. This is for information only and is not for reading aloud.

IX. RESPONSORIES

169. Its responsory follows the biblical reading in the office of readings. The text of this responsory has been drawn from traditional sources or freshly composed, in order to throw new light on the passage just read, put it in the context of the history of salvation, lead from the Old Testament to the New, turn what has been read into prayer and contemplation, or provide pleasant variety by its poetic beauty.

170. A pertinent responsory also follows the second reading. It is less closely linked with the text of the reading, however, and thus makes for a greater freedom in meditation.

171.   The responsories and the portions to be repeated even in private recitation therefore retain their value. The customary reprise of the whole responsory may be omitted when the office is not being sung, unless the sense requires this repetition.

172.   In a similar but simpler way, the responsory at morning prayer, evening prayer, and night prayer (see nos. 49 and 89), and the verse at daytime prayer, are linked to the short reading as a kind of acclamation, enabling God's word to enter more deeply into the mind and heart of the one listening or reading.

X. HYMNS AND OTHER NONBIBLICAL SONGS

173.   A very ancient tradition gives hymns the place in the office that they still retain.[12] By their mystical and poetic character they are specifically designed for God's praise. But they also are an element for the people; in fact more often than the other parts of the office the hymns bring out the proper theme of individual hours or feasts and incline and draw the spirit to a devout celebration. The beauty of their language often adds to this power. Furthermore, in the office hymns are the main poetic element created by the Church.

174.   A hymn follows the traditional rule of ending with a doxology, usually addressed to the same divine person as the hymn itself.

175.   In the office for Ordinary Time, to ensure variety, a twofold cycle of hymns is given for each hour, for use in alternate weeks.

176.   In addition, a twofold cycle of hymns has been introduced into the office of readings for Ordinary Time, one for use at night and the other for use during the day.

177.   New hymns can be set to traditional melodies of the same rhythm and meter.

178.   For vernacular celebration, the conferences of bishops may adapt the Latin hymns to suit the character of their own language and introduce fresh compositions,[13] provided these are in complete harmony with the spirit of the hour, season, or feast. Great care must be taken not to allow popular songs that have no artistic merit and are not in keeping with the dignity of the liturgy.

XI. INTERCESSIONS, LORD'S PRAYER, AND CONCLUD-
ING PRAYER

A. The Prayers or Intercessions at Morning Prayer and Evening Prayer

179.   The liturgy of the hours is a celebration in praise of God. Yet Jewish and Christian tradition does not separate prayer of petition from praise of God; often enough, praise turns somehow to petition. The Apostle Paul exhorts us to offer "prayers, petitions, intercessions, and thanksgiving for all: for kings and all in authority so that we may be able to live quiet and peaceful lives in all reverence and decency, for this is good and acceptable before God our Savior, who wishes all to be saved and to come to the knowledge of the truth" (1 Tm 2:1–4). The Fathers of the Church frequently explained this as an exhortation to offer prayer in the morning and in the evening.[14]

180.   The general intercessions, restored in the Mass of the Roman Rite, have their place also at evening prayer, though in a different fashion, as will be explained later.

181.   Since traditionally morning prayer puts the whole day in God's hands, there are invocations at morning prayer for the purpose of commending or consecrating the day to God.

182.   The word *preces* covers both the intercessions at evening prayer and the invocations for dedicating the day to God at morning prayer.

183.   In the interest of variety and especially of giving fuller expression to the many needs of the Church and of all people in relation to different states of life, groups, persons, circumstances, and seasons, different intercessory formularies are given for each day of the four-week psalter in Ordinary Time and for the special seasons of the liturgical year, as well as for certain feasts.

184.   In addition, the conferences of bishops have the right to adapt the formularies given in the book of the liturgy of the hours and also to approve new ones,[15] in accordance with the norms that follow.

185.   As in the Lord's Prayer, petitions should be linked with praise of God and acknowledgment of his glory or with a reference to the history of salvation.

186.   In the intercessions at evening prayer the last intention is always for the dead.

187.   Since the liturgy of the hours is above all the prayer of the whole Church for the whole Church, indeed for the salvation of the whole world,[16] universal intentions should take precedence over all others, namely, for: the Church and its ministers; secular authorities; the poor, the sick, and the sorrowful; the needs of the whole world, that is, peace and other intentions of this kind.

188.   It is permissible, however, to include particular intentions at both morning prayer and evening prayer.

189.   The intercessions in the office are so arranged that they can be adapted for celebration with a congregation or in a small community or for private recitation.

190.   The intercessions in a celebration with a congregation or in common are thus introduced by a brief invitation, given by the priest or minister and designating the single response that the congregation is to repeat after each petition.

191.   Further, the intentions are phrased as direct addresses to God and thus are suitable for both common celebration and private recitation.

192.   Each intention consists of two parts; the second may be used as an alternative response.

193.   Different methods can therefore be used for the intercessions. The priest or minister may say both parts of the intention and the congregation respond with a uniform response or a silent pause, or the priest or minister may say only the first part of the intention and the congregation respond with the second part.

B. Lord's Prayer

194.   In accord with ancient tradition, the Lord's Prayer has a place suited to its dignity, namely, after the intercessions at morning prayer and evening prayer, the hours most often celebrated with the people.

195.   Henceforth, therefore, the Lord's Prayer will be said with solemnity on three occasions during the day: at Mass, at morning prayer, and at evening prayer.

196.   The Lord's Prayer is said by all after a brief introduction, if this seems opportune.

C. Concluding Prayer

197.   The concluding prayer at the end marks the completion of an entire hour. In a celebration in public and with a congregation, it belongs by tradition to a priest or deacon to say this prayer.[17]

198.   In the office of readings, this prayer is as a rule the prayer proper to the day. At night prayer, the prayer is always the prayer given in the psalter for that hour.

199.   The concluding prayer at morning prayer and evening prayer is taken from the proper on Sundays, on the weekdays of the seasons of Advent, Christmas, Lent, and Easter, and on solemnities, feasts, and memorials. On weekdays in Ordinary Time the prayer is the one given in the four-week psalter to express the character of these two hours.

200.   The concluding prayer at daytime prayer is taken from the proper on Sundays, on the weekdays of the seasons of Advent, Christmas, Lent, and Easter, and on solemnities and feasts. On other days the prayers are those that express the character of the particular hour. These are given in the four-week psalter.

XII. SACRED SILENCE

201.   It is a general principle that care should be taken in liturgical services to see that "at the proper times all observe a reverent silence."[18] An opportunity for silence should therefore be provided in the celebration of the liturgy of the hours.

202.   In order to receive in our hearts the full sound of the voice of the Holy Spirit and to unite our personal prayer more closely with the word of God and the public voice of the Church, it is permissible, as occasion offers and prudence suggests, to have an interval of silence. It may come

either after the repetition of the antiphon at the end of the psalm, in the traditional way, especially if the psalm-prayer is to be said after the pause (see no. 112), or after the short or longer readings, either before or after the responsory.

Care must be taken to avoid the kind of silence that would disturb the structure of the office or annoy and weary those taking part.

203.   In individual recitation there is even greater freedom to pause in meditation on some text that moves the spirit; the office does not on this account lose its public character.

Appendix Notes

SC	Vatican Council II, *Sacrosanctum Concilium* (Constitution on the Sacred Liturgy), 4 December 1963.
SCR	Sacred Congregation of Rites.

Chapter I

1. See Acts 1:14, 4:24, 12:5 and 12. See also Eph 5:19–21.
2. See Acts 2:1–15.
3. SC art. 83.
4. See Lk 3:21–22.
5. See Lk 6:12.
6. See Mt 14:19, 15:36; Mk 6:41, 8:7; Lk 9:16; Jn 6:11.
7. See Lk 9:28–29.
8. See Mk 7:34.
9. See Jn 11:41ff.
10. See Lk 9:18.
11. See Lk 11:1.
12. See Mt 11:25ff; Lk 10:21ff.
13. See Mt 19:13.
14. See Lk 22:32.
15. See Mk 1:35, 6:46; Lk 5:16. See also Mt 4:1 and par.; Mt 14:23.
16. See Mk 1:35.
17. See Mt 14:23 and 25; Mk 6:46 and 48.
18. See Lk 6:12.
19. See Lk 4:16.
20. See Mt 21:13 and par.
21. See Mt 14:19 and par.; Mt 15:36 and par.
22. See Mt 26:26 and par.
23. See Lk 24:30.
24. See Mt 26:30 and par.
25. See Jn 12:27ff.
26. See Jn 17:1–26.
27. See Mt 26:36–44 and par.
28. See Lk 23:34 and 46; Mt 27:46; Mk 15:34.
29. See Heb 7:25.
30. Mt 5:44, 7:7, 26:41; Mk 13:33, 14:38; Lk 6:28, 10:2, 11:9, 22:40 and 46.
31. Jn 14:13ff., 15:16, 16:23ff. and 26.
32. See Mt 6:9–13; Lk 11:2–4.
33. See Lk 18:1.
34. See Lk 18:9–14.

35. See Lk 21:36; Mk 13:33.

36. See Lk 11:5–13, 18:1–8; Jn 14:13, 16:23.

37. See Mt 6:5–8, 23:14; Lk 20:47; Jn 4:23.

38. See Rom 8:15 and 26; 1 Cor 12:3; Gal 4:6; Jude 20.

39. See 2 Cor 1:20; Col 3:17.

40. See Heb 13:15.

41. See Rom 12:12; 1 Cor 7:5; Eph 6:18; Col 4:2; 1 Thes 5:17; 1 Tm 5:5; 1 Pt 4:7.

42. See 1 Tm 4:5; Jas 5:1ff.; 1 Jn 3:22, 5:14ff.

43. See Eph 5:19ff.; Heb 13:15; Rv 19:5.

44. See Col 3:17; Phil 4:6; 1 Thes 5:17; 1 Tm 2:1.

45. See Rom 8:26; Phil 4:6.

46. See Rom 15:30; 1 Tm 2:1ff.; Eph 6:18; 1 Thes 5:25; Jas 5:14 and 16.

47. See 1 Tm 2:5; Heb 8:6, 9:15, 12:24.

48. See Rom 5:2; Eph 2:18, 3:12.

49. See SC art. 83.

50. See LG no. 10.

51. Augustine, *Enarrat. in Ps. 85*, 1:CCL 39, 1176.

52. See Lk 10:21, the occasion when Jesus "rejoiced in the Holy Spirit and said: 'I thank you, Father . . . .' "

53. See Acts 2:42 Gr.

54. See Mt 6:6.

55. See SC art. 12.

56. See SC art. 83–84.

57. See SC art. 88.

58. SC art. 94.

59. See PO no. 5.

60. CD no. 30.

61. SC art. 5.

62. See SC art. 83 and 98.

63. SC art. 7.

64. See SC art. 10.

65. SC art. 33.

66. See SC art. 24.

67. See SC art. 33.

68. 1 Thes 5:17.

69. See Heb 13:15.

70. SC art. 84.

71. SC art. 85.

72. See SC art. 83.

73. LG no. 50; SC art. 8 and 104.
74. LG no. 48.
75. See Rom 8:19.
76. See SC art. 83.
77. See Heb 5:7.
78. See PO no. 6.
79. See LG no. 41.
80. See no. 24 of this Instruction.
81. See PC no. 7.
82. SC art. 10.
83. SC art. 2.
84. See Jn 15:5.
85. See SC art. 86.
86. See Eph 2:21–22.
87. See Eph 4:13.
88. See SC art. 2.
89. See SC art. 90. *Rule of St. Benedict* ch. 19.
90. See PO no. 14; OT no. 8.

[R1]Query: When a person recites the liturgy of the hours, do the readings have to be pronounced or simply read? Reply: *It is enough simply to read them.* The conciliar Constitution on the Liturgy says nothing about an obligation to oral recitation when a person says the office alone, although there was a difference of opinion on this among the conciliar Fathers. They decreed a reform of the breviary not for the purpose of shortening the time for prayer but of giving all who celebrate the liturgy of the hours a better time for prayer. Accordingly, all the documents treating of the reform of the divine office urge that "the mind be attuned to the voice" and that "the prayer of the Church be a source of devotion and nourishment also for personal prayer" (SC art. 90). This calls for the reading of Scripture and the Fathers as well as the recitation of the psalms, in which God is speaking to his people and they are responding (see SC art. 33), to consist "not in a cursory reading of a breviary" (see Schema of SC, *Modi a Patribus Conciliaribus propositi, a Commissione de sacra Liturgia examinati* vol. 4, *De Officio Divino*, 13) but in personal meditation. Otherwise even if there is a recitation of the hours, there is no penetration by the word of God nor true prayer. The true course is "that as we celebrate the office, we must recognize our own voices echoing in Christ, his voice echoing in us" (Paul VI, Ap. Const. *Laudis canticum*). This is the way for the liturgy of the hours to be a personal prayer, sincere and effective, a source of devotion, the sustenance of the spiritual life and of each day's apostolic labors. Then the relationship between the Church's prayer and personal prayer is strengthened and mental prayer has an unfailing source in the readings, the psalms, and other parts of the liturgy of the hours (see ibid.). Sometimes a surer guarantee for this objective of the liturgy of the hours in individual recitation may be to omit the oral recitation of each word, especially in the case of the readings: Not 9 (1973) 150.

91. See SC art. 26.

92. See SC art. 41.

93. CD no. 11.

94. See art. 42. See also AA no. 10.

95. See SC art. 26 and 84.

96. See AG no. 17.

97. CD no. 15.

98. See SC art. 100.

99. See PO no. 5.

100. See nos. 100–109 of this Instruction.

101. CD no. 33; see also PC nos. 6, 7, 15; AG no. 15.

102. See SC art. 99.

103. See SC art. 100.

104. See Jn 4:23.

105. See GE no. 2; AA no. 16.

106. See AA no. 11.

107. See PO no. 13.

108. See SC art. 41; LG no. 21.

109. See LG no. 26; CD no. 15.

110. See PO no. 13.

111. See PO no. 5.

112. See Jn 10:11, 17:20 and 23.

113. See SC art. 90.

114. See LG no. 41.

114(b). *Code of Canon Law*, can. 276 §§2, 3 and can. 1174 §1.

115. See DV no. 25; PO no. 13.

116. See *Code of Canon Law*, can. 276 §§2, 3. Paul VI, Motu Proprio *Sacrum Diaconatus Ordinem*, 18 June 1967, no. 27.

[R2] Query: What should the arrangement be in celebrating the liturgy of the hours in cathedral chapters? Reply: The GILH nos. 76 and 31 regulate the celebration of the liturgy of the hours in chapters of canons: "[Text quoted, nos. 76 and 31]." Particular law is to determine in detail which hours must be celebrated by the chapter; the individual members who are absent from the capitular celebration must recite such hours privately. The greatest care is to be taken to celebrate the hours at the corresponding natural time of day, with solemnity and the participation of the people. There is to be no combining of more than one hour at the same celebration. Now that the GILH has been published, it is required that the practice of chapters be made to conform to it. If necessary there is to be a revision of the capitular statutes and approval by the authority competent to give it. The aim is that the service to the liturgy rendered by the chapter reflect the documents of the liturgical reform: Not 8 (1972) 192.

117. See SCR, Instr. InterOec no. 78b.
118. See SC art. 95.
119. See Acts 4:32.
120. See SC art. 100.
121. See SC art. 26, 28–30.
122. See SC art. 27.

Chapter II

1. See Heb 3:7–4:16.
2. SC art. 89 a; see also art. 100.
3. Basil the Great, *Regulae fusius tractatae* resp. 37, 3: PG 31, 1014.
4. Cyprian, *De oratione dominica* 35: PL 4, 561.
5. Basil the Great, *Regulae fusius tractatae* resp. 37, 3: PG 31, 1015.
6. See Ps 141:2.
7. John Cassian, *De institutione coenob.* 3, 3: PL 49, 124, 125.
8. Cyprian, *De oratione dominica* 35: PL 4, 560.
9. RP, Ordination of Priests no. 14.
10. Ambrose, *De officiis ministrorum* 1, 20, 88: PL 16, 50. See also DV no. 25.
11. SC art. 89 c.
12. Augustine, *Sermo Guelferbytanus* 5: PL Suppl 2, 550.
13. Ibid.: PL Suppl 2, 552.
14. See SC art. 89.
15. See SC art. 38.

Chapter III

1. SC art. 90.
2. *Rule of St. Benedict* ch. 19.

3. See *Rule of St. Benedict* ch. 19.

4. See Mt 22:44ff.

5. See SC art. 91.

6. SC art. 102.

7. Gregory the Great, *Homilia 34 in Evangelia*: PL 76: 1282.

8. See SC art. 38.

9. Vincent of Lerins, *Commonitorium* 2: PL 50, 640.

10. Bernard of Clairvaux, *Sermo 3 in vigilia Nativitatis* 1: PL 183 (ed. 1879) 94.

11. See SC art. 92 c.

12. See SC art. 93.

13. See SC art. 38.

14. Thus, for example, John Chrysostom, *In Epist. ad Tim 1*, Homilia 6: PG 62, 530.

15. See SC art. 38.

16. See SC art. 83 and 89.

17. See no. 256 of this Instruction.

18. SC art. 30.